WESTERN
TO THE COAST

IMAGES FROM THE TRANSPORT TREASURY ARCHIVE

COMPILED BY JEFFERY GRAYER

The
· Transport ·
Treasury

ISBN 978-1-913251-21-5

First Published in 2022 by Transport Treasury Publishing Ltd.,
16 Highworth Close, High Wycombe, HP13 7PJ

www.ttpublishing.co.uk

Printed in the UK by Henry Ling Limited at the Dorset Press, Dorchester, DT1 1HD

Information from the 1947 guide was sourced from the Railway Studies Library at Newton Abbot where several copies of these guides are held together with an extensive collection of railway literature. This library was instigated by David St. John Thomas, co-founder of David & Charles, the publishing house previously based in the town.

Front Cover: Where else could possibly feature on the front cover of a book about Western Region coastal resorts than the famous sea wall section between Dawlish and Teignmouth where 6800 Class No. 6878 "Longford Grange" has charge of a down stopping passenger working at the height of the summer season on 14th. July 1958. The driver, cap in hand, poses for the photographer none other than Dick Riley. *R12258*

Frontispiece:
The attractive branch line station of Fowey, terminus of the service from the main line at Lostwithiel, is graced by the presence of 4500 Class No. 5572 in this undated view. There appears to be a reasonable number of passengers but the primary function of the line was to handle china clay traffic and it remains open to Carne Point at the present time for this freight. Originally there was another line serving Fowey from St. Blazey but this closed to passengers back in 1929 and to freight in July 1968 at which time it was converted to a private road for the exclusive use of clay lorries operating between Par and the docks in Fowey. *NS201248A*

Rear Cover:
A delightful period scene showing No. 2906 "Lady of Lynn" traversing this scenic stretch of the WR main line having just emerged from Clerk's tunnel, one of five on this section of the route between Dawlish and Teignmouth. Constructed in May 1906 this was one of the second series of the original Saint class 4-6-0s, comprising ten locomotives numbered 2901–10 and named after historical, mythological or poetical 'Ladies'. Googling the name "Lady of Lynn" the only reference I can find is to a novel of Walter Besant published in 1901 where the lady in question turns out to be a "three masted, full rigged ship of 380 tons" so perhaps "fictional ships" should be added to the categories of Saint names! These locomotives were superseded on express duties by the Castle class as far back as the 1920s and 1930s hence the use of a Saint here on a rather mundane 4 coach local of clerestory stock. Intriguingly one of the coupling rods surviving from No. 2906 was utilised in the new build Saint "Lady of Legend". *GW147*

Contents

Introduction

Dorset - Weymouth, Portland, Abbotsbury, Bridport, West Bay — 5

Devon - Starcross, Dawlish Warren, Dawlish, Teignmouth, Torquay, Paignton, Churston, Brixham, Kingswear, Dartmouth, Kingsbridge, Plymouth, Barnstaple — 12

Cornwall - Saltash, Looe, Fowey, Par, Penryn, Falmouth, Hayle, Marazion, Penzance, Lelant, Carbis Bay, St. Ives, Perranporth, St. Agnes, Newquay — 42

Somerset - Minehead, Watchet, Weston-Super-Mare, Clevedon, Portishead — 71

Gloucestershire - Severn Beach — 84

South Wales - Penarth, Barry Island, Porthcawl — 86

West Wales - Ferryside, Tenby — 90

Mid Wales - Cardigan, Aberystwyth, Borth, Towyn — 93

North Wales - Barmouth, Harlech, Portmadoc, Cricceth, Penychain, Pwllheli — 100

Gateway to Cornwall and the fabled Riviera – the Royal Albert Bridge at Saltash, one of Brunel's finest achievements, neatly framed by the arches of Coombe viaduct some 70 years ago in the spring of 1952.

Introduction

Following the publication of "**Southern to the Coast**" in 2021, this companion volume focuses attention on some of the numerous coastal resorts served by trains of the Western Region (WR). Once again use is made of the "Holiday Haunts" guides published initially by the Great Western Railway (GWR) and later by British Railways (BR). In this instance the final GWR publication for 1947 has been consulted and over fifty coastal towns served by the GWR/WR have been chosen for inclusion in this book. Following the format of the previous volume, introductory descriptions taken from this guide are used to preface each resort, thereby giving a period flavour which is also enhanced by the inclusion of examples of the publicity of the period produced by local Tourist Information offices advertising the delights and amenities of each location. It is an interesting reflection of the times that the 1947 guide felt it important to draw the attention of holidaymakers to the nature of the subsoil, the availability of a good supply of drinking water and the religious denominations catered for in each resort. One also finds references to the recent war and the damage inflicted by air raids. The first "Holiday Haunts" produced by the GWR in 1906 and costing 1d proved to be the forerunner of an eventual total of 32 editions culminating in this final one produced before nationalisation for the 1947 holiday season. In addition to descriptive text there were copious photographs, many of which were taken by the company's own photographers from the Engineering Department as their work took them to all points of the network. Dealing with the many thousands of advertisements included in these publications for hotels, B&Bs and camping sites was a herculean task with a great many staff involved. The guides proved enormously popular with the public as evidenced by the fact that the print run of 40,000 recorded in 1921 had risen to 175,000 just six years later.

As with the Southern, a number of named trains, originating from the WR's London terminus of Paddington, served the coastal resorts including the "Cornish Riviera", "Torbay Express", "Royal Duchy", "Mayflower", "Pembroke Coast Express" and the "Cambrian Coast Express". These were supplemented by holiday expresses from the Midlands and the North such as the "Devonian" and the "Cornishman". Although fortunately a number of the branch lines serving coastal resorts are still with us today, including those to Looe, Falmouth, Newquay, St. Ives, Barry and Tenby, there have naturally been casualties and resorts such as Aberaeron, Cardigan, Porthcawl, Clevedon, Brixham and Kingsbridge are no longer rail served. However, preservation has played its part in ensuring that at least two coastal towns served by the former GWR, Minehead and Kingswear for Dartmouth, continue to see trains in the 21st Century.

The vast Transport Treasury archive of more than half a million images has again been scoured to find the 160 views included here and although many of these photographs are little more than 60 years old they represent an age so different in many respects from this, the third decade of the 21st Century. It has often been said that "Nostalgia is not what it used to be" but I wonder how many of us would dearly swap the hustle and bustle of modern life for the seemingly calmer pre-pandemic times of the 1950s and early 1960s and enjoy again the sight and sound of holiday trains steaming towards the coast packed with excited holidaymakers looking forward to their annual break.

A wide variety of motive power is featured here from top link express locomotives such as "Kings" and "Castles" to the less exotic "Hall", "Grange", "Manor" and "County" types. At the other end of the spectrum are the branch line locomotives, epitomised in the humble Prairie tank, which often took the holidaymaker over the last few miles of their trip to journey's end at some sleepy seaside terminus. The Western's own idiosyncratic diesel hydraulic types are also not overlooked and "Warships" and "Hymeks" feature as does the ubiquitous DMU. Once passengers had arrived at their destination, providing of course that they were not heartily sick of rail travel by that time, they might well avail themselves of one of the many "Holiday Runabout" tickets which, between April and October, gave one week's unlimited travel in a specified area. For the sum of 18/6 in 1958 for example, one could travel from Penzance to Par encompassing the St. Ives, Helston, Falmouth and both branches that then served Newquay. Even though this ticket came with the proviso that neither travel on the "Cornish Riviera" express nor on road motors was permitted, and that no allowance could be made for the lack of a Sunday service on some routes, it still represented outstanding value for money and for an additional charge, trips on River Fal vessels from Falmouth to Truro operated by Victory Pleasures Ltd. could also be enjoyed.

Beginning in Dorset, where the tourist spoils of the principal resort of Weymouth were shared with the Southern Region, we journey through South Devon to Cornwall and then on through Somerset and briefly Gloucestershire before covering South, West and Mid Wales and ending at the WR outpost of Pwllheli in North Wales. As with the previous volume, some "estuarine" rather than strictly coastal resorts such as Kingsbridge, Barnstaple, Ferryside and Cardigan have been included. Following the lockdowns of recent times the British seaside resort has experienced something of a renaissance with foreign holiday travel proving problematic and those UK destinations retaining rail access have no doubt counted themselves particularly fortunate.

Jeffery Grayer
Devon

2022

Dorset

WEYMOUTH

Amusements: New Pier bandstand, Concert Hall, Cinemas. Recreations: golf, yachting (Headquarters of the Royal Dorset Yacht Club), bathing, boating, angling, tennis bowls, putting, cricket, etc.
Neither its constant increase of population, nor the bombing experienced during the war, could destroy the charm of Weymouth's great bay and the curve of its superb seafront with the many delightful Georgian houses. It was at Weymouth that Ralph Allen, of Bath, first introduced sea bathing, later popularised by King George III.

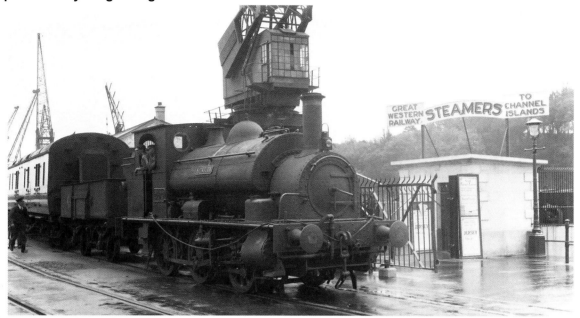

Above: A real piece of history to begin our trip around the coastal resorts served by the Western. As the sign indicates "GWR Steamers to the Channel Islands" this can only be Weymouth Quay, seen here in about 1935. The veteran 0-6-0ST "Kidwelly", seen toying with a wagon and coach at the quay station, dated from 1903 having been constructed for the Burry Port & Gwendraeth Valley Railway in South Wales by Avonside. Passing to the GWR at the Grouping in 1923 together with sister locomotive "Cwm Mawr" they were put to work at Weymouth Quay. "Kidwelly", now renumbered 2194, left Weymouth in 1940 but lasted in traffic mainly in the Taunton area until withdrawal under BR in 1953. Channel Islands boat trains ran from both Paddington and Waterloo direct to Weymouth Quay, although from the 1960 season onwards the service was concentrated on the SR route. *NS209998*

Overleaf Top: This 1955 view of a locomotive on the turntable of the Weymouth Miniature Railway is interesting from two aspects, firstly it illustrates one of the attractions for holidaymakers often to be found at seaside resorts and in the background is the girder bridge of the Backwater Viaduct crossing Radipole Lake and carrying the Portland branch away from Weymouth. The 10 ¼" WMR line was constructed in 1947 by Baydon Miniature Railways, one of several seaside railways they operated during that era. It ran beside Radipole Lake for about 500m, looped round and headed back to the station. It proved to be an instant success, carrying 100,000 passengers in 1950 for example. The railway was operated initially by three steam locomotives, all 4-4-2s and built by David Curwen, one being turned out in an unusual cream livery and named "Merrie England". The enterprise went through several subsequent owners, switching to diesel power, but in its later years became rather run down, being eventually closed in 1979 when the track was removed. It went through a further manifestation in 1980 as a 15" gauge line but this only lasted a few months before closing for good. The vintage motor coach seen on the left enhances this scene of yesteryear. *AEB924*

Overleaf Bottom: The exterior of Weymouth station is seen here in September 1965, the original station buildings having been designed by T. H. Bertram and constructed in timber with a glazed overall roof across the tracks which was removed after WW2. Due to rapid growth after the war the station underwent a major expansion in the late 1950s gaining two lengthy excursion platforms, additional sidings and a new signal box. However, with the subsequent decline in traffic in the 1960s the station was progressively rationalised, particularly so after the end of steam-hauled operations in 1967 with the goods yard closing in 1972 and the signal box and most of the remaining sidings being taken out of use in 1987. The current station, opened in July 1986, is but a mere shadow of its former self. A "G.R." postbox and a couple of vans of the period complete the scene. *LRF1987*

CHANNEL ISLANDS
Via WEYMOUTH

1st and 2nd Class Rail and Steamer

OUTWARDS		Mondays to Fridays until 19th September, 1958, inclusive	Tuesdays, Thursdays and Saturdays only to 23rd September, to 1st November, 1958, inclusive, only	Saturday, 20th September, 1958	FOR DETAILS OF SERVICE ARRANGEMENTS AFTER 1st NOVEMBER, 1958, SEE LATER ANNOUNCEMENTS
London (Paddington).. dep		am 8R20	pm 6R 0	am 8R30	
Weymouth Quay .. { arr		pm 12 17	10 47	pm 12 18	
{ dep		1 0	am 2N 0	1 0	
Guernsey .. .. { arr		5 15	7N 0	5 15	
{ dep		5 45	7N30	5 45	
Jersey .. .. arr		7 45	9N30	7 45	

N—Following morning   R—Restaurant Car Paddington to Weymouth

PORTLAND
Beach: pebbles.
The rocky Isle of Portland, tethered to the mainland by the extraordinary barrier of pebbles known as Chesil Beach, well repays exploration. It has several quaint little villages, castle ruins, giant cliffs and many ancient customs peculiar to the islanders.

There was precious little left of Portland station apart from these bare platforms by the time that this RCTS "Greyhound Railtour" of the 14th August 1960 visited the site hauled by pannier tank No. 3737 with three Bulleid coaches in tow. The platforms remained in situ until the 1970s when the whole area was absorbed into one of the surrounding military establishments. A photographic stop on the railtour was made here before continuing on to the terminus at Easton. The return to London via Broadstone, West Moors and Salisbury was courtesy of T9 No. 30718 as far as Salisbury whence L Class No. 31768 took over for the run up to the capital. *WS4907*

CONVEYANCE OF PASSENGERS' LUGGAGE.

IN order to prevent loss of or delay to luggage, passengers are requested to see that all old labels are removed or defaced, and that the packages are fully and legibly addressed. For further security it is suggested the owner's full name and address be placed inside the package.

ABBOTSBURY

Early closing: Thursday.

Abbotsbury, an old world village sheltered by grassy hills, has some ancient buildings but a still greater attraction for tourists is the great swannery, now the property of the Earl of Ilchester, which is open from April to September. Over a thousand swans nest there every spring.

Above: No. 1403 waits in the pouring rain on the final morning of services on the cold and windy 29th November 1952. Morning trains were worked by No. 1403 and the weather did not improve during the day when the final journey, the 8:25pm from Abbotsbury with two auto trailers and 140 passengers, was hauled by classmate No.1453 suitably adorned with a wreath. Except for a few workers and schoolchildren on the early train and their return at teatime very few people made any regular use of the train with less than 6 passengers carried per journey and only 500 tickets / month on average being sold at Abbotsbury, although this did rise to 749 in August when over 1,300 tickets were collected that month. *RCR3821*

Below: By July 1956 this was the scene at Abbotsbury where track had been removed from the branch during 1954/55. Track removal took nearly a year due to floods experienced during July 1955 following a record quantity of rain – 11 inches – falling in one day. Although the station building at Abbotsbury was subsequently demolished, being replaced by a bungalow and garage which now stands on the former platform, the Goods Shed seen in the background to this view remains in situ today. *RCR75738*

BRIDPORT & WEST BAY
Population 6,000. Altitude 50 to 200 feet.

Bridport is a busy market town with an eventful history. Its harbour, a diminutive marine parade, and a bathing beach are at West Bay a mile and a half away. The famous George Inn, at which Charles II lay in hiding, is now a chemist's shop.

The signalman descends the steps from his box whilst Collett 5700 Class pannier tank No. 7749 awaits departure time with its two coach B set for the junction at Maiden Newton on an unrecorded date in 1954. The box would remain operational until June 1965 when track rationalisation left just a single line serving one platform at Bridport. *NS200591*

Opposite Top: Single "Bubble Car" unit No. W55033W waits at the much rationalised Bridport station which was now unstaffed with the whole line operating very much as a "basic railway". DMUs had virtually replaced steam working on the branch from the start of the 1959 summer service and although the 2 car units initially supplied were later supplanted by just a single car, the branch remarkably survived until 1975 and I vividly remember taking a final ride during the penultimate weekend of operation in April of that year. The Pressed Steel unit seen here, constructed in 1960, achieved fame as being the final such unit to work over the Bridport line and it has been preserved and can be found today on the Colne Valley Railway. *ICSD1432*

Opposite Bottom: Far more convenient for Bridport town centre was East Street station, seen here on 4th July 1961 during the freight only existence of the West Bay extension line, some 31 years after withdrawal of the passenger service back in 1930. The station building was occupied at the time hence the barrier and garden gate fencing it off from the platform edge. From December 1962 the extension line was closed to freight traffic which latterly had consisted of just a few wagonloads of coal and some beach shingle, and much of the route was swallowed up in the Bridport by-pass. *RCR15983*

Above: The end of the line at West Bay terminus, seen on 25th August 1963, is looking very down at heel some two years after the final freight service had departed. This was the occasion of the final special train to work over the line sponsored by the Southern Counties Touring Society which featured pannier tanks Nos. 7782 and 4689 hauling 7 coaches. A small crowd has obviously gathered to witness this spectacle but it was a sad end for the hopes of the founding railway company that West Bay would develop into a thriving coastal resort. *LRF7877*

Devon

STARCROSS

Early closing: Thursday.

Starcross, set along the coast road from Exeter to Dawlish, beside the estuary of the Exe, is the South Devon starting point for the ferry to Exmouth and East Devon. It is within 1¾ miles of the picturesque village of Kenton and Powderham Castle seat of the Earls of Devon which stands in a fine park. Flowers are cultivated extensively in the neighbourhood including acres of fragrant violets.

Below: "Starcross for Exmouth" reads the running in board as an unidentified prairie tank prepares to leave the station bunker first on 2nd September 1958 with a local service to Exeter. The pier, at the end of which lies the ferry to Exmouth, can be seen beyond the railings of the down platform. In the distance the pumping house tower of Brunel's ill fated atmospheric railway experiment can just be glimpsed above the up platform awning. The ferry which crosses the Exe in just 15 minutes still operates today, generally between April and October, and saves some twenty miles of rail journey between the two towns. *PY100315*

GLORIOUS DEVON

Posed rather uncomfortably on jagged rocks, this "Holiday Haunts" bathing belle advertising the delights of Glorious Devon seems quite at ease bizarrely doing some knitting! Perhaps another rather fetching woollen one piece bathing cozzie?

DAWLISH WARREN

There is a golf course on the sand dunes at Dawlish Warren which also attracts bathers and picnickers and a ferry from Starcross links the Warren with Exmouth. The valleys of the Teign and Exe are within easy reach.

Above: In this 1930s view an unidentified Class 4300 mogul runs past the goods yard, opened in 1912, and takes the platform line on entry to Dawlish Warren station where through running lines for non-stop services were provided. The station was well sited to give access to the beach, amusements, holiday camps and later mobile home sites that today proliferate in the area. A packed car park full of fascinating vehicles of the period can be seen on the seaward side of the line. *GW297*

Overleaf Top: Although originally introduced in 1931 for use in the London suburban area, nine well loaded coaches was undoubtedly a bit of a stretch for 6100 Class No. 6166 as it gets away from the Dawlish Warren stop and rounds the curve by Langstone Rock on 19th August 1959 with an augmented local service for Torquay. In the distance rakes of camping coaches can be seen by the station to the left of the original station's footbridge, built in 1873, there being at one time no less than nine such vehicles parked here. *PH000499*

Overleaf Bottom: From the top of the aforementioned Langstone Rock, which provided a magnificent vantage point for railway photography, Castle Class No. 5071 "Spitfire" has charge of the service on 28th August 1954 which carried reporting number 708 indicating a Saturdays only train from Carmarthen to Penzance. Crowds are out on the beach and on the trackside walk no doubt enjoying the apparently glorious summer weather. *RCR5290*

DAWLISH

Subsoil: red sandstone. Climate: cool in summer, warm in winter.

Even from the train it is easy to realise the attractions of Dawlish as a family resort and closer acquaintance only heightens its charm. It lies on the south coast of the true Red Devon where the colouring of the cliffs is so brilliant that the sands and even the ripples of the incoming tide have a pink tinge. Its shops are set well back around a long central green where a stream cascades under ornamental bridges in a pretty garden.

Heading south west out of Dawlish station are a brace of Hall Class 4-6-0s, No.4930 "Hagley Hall", now preserved on the Severn Valley Railway, and No. 4982 "Acton Hall", a recent re-allocation to Plymouth Laira depot, towards the end of the 1961 summer season on 9th September. Again, the station was well sited for both beach and town and passengers enjoyed a grandstand view of the coast from the train, stretching all the way from Dawlish Warren to Teignmouth. *FW12-2*

Opposite Top: Entering Dawlish from the west comes an unidentified Castle Class carrying train reporting number 949 which, depending upon the date of this undated view, could either be the 8am (SO) from Paignton - Manchester or the 8am (SX) Plymouth to Crewe. The milepost showing 206 ¼ miles from London reflects the "Great Way Round" via Bristol. The Gaiety restaurant and snack bar seen on the far right, which advertises dancing, is a distinctive building with its twin turrets which today functions as a B&B establishment but almost certainly dancing is not on the menu! *PH000213*

Opposite Bottom: No. 5029 "Nunney Castle" passes the distinctive signal box at Dawlish under the watchful eye of the signalman before coming to a halt at the station with an unidentified up express in August 1959. After some six months based at Newton Abbot in 1959 the 4-6-0 was transferred to Laira before what was to be its final move to Cardiff East Dock from where it was withdrawn in December 1963 and fortunately sold to Woodham's at Barry in South Wales. After a sojourn here of some twelve years, it was rescued for preservation in May 1976 and is currently operated by Jeremy Hosking's Locomotive Services Ltd. and has been a frequent performer on the main line. *PH000211*

Above: Passing a steam hauled local heading west on 9th September 1961, Warship class D810 "Cockade" powers away from Dawlish under the red sandstone cliffs with a Plymouth/Paignton to Paddington service, the two portions having been combined at Newton Abbot. *FW12-5D*

THE SEA WALL BETWEEN DAWLISH AND TEIGNMOUTH

Eschewing the temptation to employ that much overused word "iconic", perhaps nothing epitomises the scenic beauties of the coastline served by the Western Region than that stretch of track between Dawlish Warren and Teignmouth in South Devon which was, as it remains today, a favourite location for railway photographers. Having the convenience of a lineside walk separating the main line from the sea, this was an ideal spot to capture those holiday expresses as they sped westwards and even with today's rather monotonous diet of diesel traction the attractiveness of this section remains largely unaltered.

Above: Powering along the base of the cliffs between Teignmouth and Dawlish comes Warship classmate D806 "Cambrian" with a service from Plymouth to Manchester (London Road) on 14th July 1959. This locomotive, which had entered service only a month before on 3rd June, was still looking resplendent in its shining new paintwork - a far cry indeed from the work stained appearance of the last few examples of the class in later years. *RCR 13873*

Below: Coming in the opposite direction, on that same July day in 1959 and having just emerged from the 512 yards of Parson's tunnel, comes 5100 Class No. 4117 with a down local service. When the original single line was doubled west of Parson's tunnel a signal box was provided here in 1884. The line east to Dawlish through the tunnel was not doubled until 1905 and in 1909 the signal box was boarded up out of use. However, due to the increase in summer traffic, the box was reinstated in 1934 but thirty years later in 1964 it was closed permanently and later demolished. Today one can still walk down the aptly named Smugglers' Lane, as the former signalmen must have done to reach this isolated box, in order to access the sea wall here. *RCR13875*

Above: As the headboard and reporting number testify, this is a superb shot of the down "Cornishman" in full cry as it passes Sprey Point which had the added attraction for railway photographers and the public alike of the cafe serving TEAS as advertised on the side of the building seen on the right. The locomotive, which obviously has steam to spare judging by the white plume emanating from the safety valves made more dramatic by the dark backdrop, is Castle Class No. 5071 "Spitfire" and the date is 19th July 1956. *RCR7748*

Below: On the same day, and slowing for the curves on the approach to Teignmouth station, is Britannia pacific No. 70024 "Vulcan". Reporting number 100 indicates that this is the 5.30 am from Paddington to Penzance via Bristol. Although seen here with an 81A shedcode, Old Oak Common, Plymouth Laira depot had received four Britannias (Nos. 70021-24) from new in 1951 followed by No. 70025 in 1952. No. 70024 remained at Plymouth until the end of 1956 when it was transferred to Cardiff Canton depot. *RCR7732*

TEIGNMOUTH

Subsoil: shingle. Beach: sandy. Churches: CofE, RC, Methodist, Congregational, Baptist, Plymouth Brethren.

Teignmouth lies on that famous stretch of the Red Devon coast and attracts the notice of every traveller on the GWR main line to Penzance but is so hidden away behind its red cliffs and wooded hills that it is necessary to explore it thoroughly before it can be appreciated fully. Its seafront has a pier, a promenade and flower gardens and a pavilion which seats 800. A long bridge across the estuary of the River Teign gives access to the little village of Shaldon and the coast to Tor Bay.

Above: Exeter based Hall Class No. 5976 "Ashwicke Hall" rounds the curve out of Teignmouth with an unidentified up passenger working on 2nd July 1957. The tower of St. Michael the Archangel is prominent in this panorama which reveals some of Teignmouth's attractive seafront and it was in this church that yachtsman Donald Crowhurst had one of his final photographs taken the day before setting off on his ill fated round the world solo attempt in his craft named "Teignmouth Electron" in 1968. *RCR10923*

Opposite Top: It is such a photogenic spot that one could be forgiven for including another view of the curve out of Teignmouth, this time graced by Britannia pacific No. 70021 "Morning Star" with train number 273, the 7:30 am Penzance to Crewe service, on 19th July 1956. Following an accident at Milton in Berkshire in 1955 involving classmate No. 70026, where handrails on the smoke deflectors were deemed to have obscured the driver's view, these were later removed and replaced with hand holds cut out of the deflectors on all of the type then allocated to the Western Region. However, this does not seem to have occurred yet with No. 70021, seen here with original handrails still in situ. *RCR7733*

Opposite Bottom: The up "Devonian", which was a restaurant car service operating between Paignton and Bradford (Forster Square), is seen here getting away from Teignmouth at 10 am, if running to time, in the charge of Castle Class No. 5055 "Earl of Eldon" on 17th July 1958. This image illustrates the length of the down platform then in use but which is now overgrown and out of bounds to passengers. *RCR12316*

Above: On 9th September 1961 Castle Class No. 4077 "Chepstow Castle" runs into Teignmouth with a Cardiff to Kingswear service carrying the chalked reporting number C29. The adoption of a letter in front of the reporting number had occurred the previous year and was the first stage in the implementation of a nationwide train numbering system with the WR being the first to adopt the new system. The down platform at Teignmouth extending in this view beyond the overbridge has today, as previously mentioned, been shortened and passengers can now only alight on the section of platform on the station side of the bridge. *FW14-3*

Below: On 14th July 1958 the down noon Paddington – Kingswear "Torbay Express" is seen passing the Old Quay signal box at Teignmouth where a line to the docks ran off to the right. Castle Class No. 5034 "Corfe Castle" heads the train over the points leading to the quay which had its own motive power in the shape of a Sentinel steam tractor named "The Elephant", fitted with large wooden buffers for manoeuvring wagons on the quay. BR scheduled the quay sidings for closure in 1967 due mainly to the establishment of a new coal concentration depot at Exmouth Junction which removed the requirement for coal to be delivered through the docks in Teignmouth. It is believed the box closed sometime in the late 1960s. *RCR12261*

TORQUAY

Parks, etc.: Over 1,000 acres. Marine spa treatment for rheumatism, arthritis, sciatica, lumbago and allied ailments.

Although by far the largest of the purely holiday towns of Devon, Torquay is a town which has a power of captivating every beholder instantly. Its special charm is an air of immaculate, well cared for beauty allied to the natural loveliness of the miles of cliff walks and drives. Terraced on wooded hills overlooking no less than eight principal beaches, Torquay provides all, and more than all, the entertainment and sports demanded by modern holiday makers all through the year with hundreds of hotels to suit every purse. The Marine Spa offers 37 different British and Continental treatments under qualified supervision. The corporation has not only preserved miles of cliff walks from Meadfoot Bay to Anstey's Cove, Babbacombe and Oddicombe, but in 1934 purchased all the coastline from Oddicombe to Labrador to save it from unwise development. The floodlighting and illuminations are colourful and popular and have been extended recently.

HOLIDAY COMFORTS ASSURED...

The Bungalow Hotel has long been acclaimed for peaceful comfort and attentive service. Overlooking beautiful Torbay, and within the lovely grounds of the Imperial Hotel, it is conveniently situated for visiting the numerous beauty spots in and around Torquay. It is also near to the town's shopping and entertainments centre.

Being under the same direction as the Imperial Hotel, visitors can daily enjoy dancing, squash, tennis, miniature golf, or billiards at that famous hotel without extra charge. Tariff from Miss L. RICHARDS, Manageress.

Bungalow HOTEL
TORQUAY

The "Torbay Express" is seen in its spiritual home of Torquay and, in a view believed to date from 1959, King Class No. 6024 "King Edward I" with reporting number 520 gets its five coach load, the small amount of stock indicating that possibly this is a wintertime service, under way for the subsequent stops of Paignton, Churston (for Brixham) and Kingswear (for Dartmouth). This fine locomotive was to be withdrawn in June 1962 having by that time been displaced by diesel traction on such prestigious services. However, it was saved for posterity and can now be found on the West Somerset Railway where it is undergoing an extensive overhaul. *NS201117*

Above: Humbler locomotive fare was also on offer at Torquay where Exeter based Collett 5100 Class 2-6-2T No. 4117 has charge of a local down service. The width between the platforms clearly indicates the broad gauge origins of the layout here and the current station dates from 1878 when signal boxes were provided at each end, the southern one still remaining in situ today. *NS20117A*

Below: The exterior view of the ornate station building, built of local grey rubblestone, remains much the same today although of course the cars of the period have been replaced by more modern variants. The station was listed in 1986 and plans are currently in hand to install lifts in the two footbridge towers to improve disabled access. A mayoral suggestion to designate the station as "Torquay Seafront" and to rename Torre station as "Torquay" made some years ago appears to have come to nothing. Period advertisements are always of interest and those visible on the end wall seem to be directed towards drinkers with Guinness and Simonds "For a man sized thirst" apparently, prominent. Simonds brewery, founded in Reading in 1785, specialised in pale ale and amalgamated with Courage in 1960, dropping the Simonds name ten years later. *LRF4883*

PAIGNTON

Altitude: rising to 612 feet. Foreshore: sandy. Subsoil: Devon red sandstone. Churches: CofE, Non conformist, R.C., Spiritualist.

Paignton is run on modern lines with fine hotels along the seafront, spacious promenades laid out with lawns and flowerbeds, and long stretches of sand on which there are bathing huts and tents. Paignton has a full programme of amusements during the season ranging from a regatta in August, athletic meetings, aquatic galas, and bowling and tennis tournaments to concerts and carnivals. The Primley Zoo, a mile out of the town, is a great attraction with its wide range of animals and birds, tea gardens, rare tropical plants and flowers and a toy railway. A short cliff walk past Paignton Harbour leads to the splendid Goodrington Sands. Just prior to the war £54,000 was spent on improvements at Goodrington which included new cliff gardens, promenades, provision for additional sites for seaside cabins and huts, up to date bathing stations, putting greens, a large boating lake, model yacht sailing ponds, a Peter Pan playground, attractive cafes and tea gardens, and beautifully laid out flower and rose gardens and shrubberies.

With the up platform packed with waiting passengers, Hall Class No. 4967 "Shirenewton Hall" runs light engine through the station on 7th September 1957. On the left can be seen the carriage sidings where stock is berthed awaiting their return trips and which today are occupied by the Torbay Steam Railway which continues to offer services beyond Paignton to Kingswear. *PY10005P*

CHURSTON

Early closing: Thursday

Churston has many scattered villas and a secluded bathing beach but its chief attraction is its splendid 18 hole golf course on the cliffs above Torbay.

Below: Hauling the 1:50 pm from Kingswear on 3rd June 1960, No. 1007 "County of Brecknock" is signalled away from the down platform at Churston on to the Up Main as shown by the route indicator situated by the starting signal. It looks as if the driver was waiting until the photographer, seen camera in hand, had taken his shot before getting his mount under way. *H1506*

Opposite Top: Busy times at Churston as one of the footplate crew of No. 4117, which is running in underneath the overbridge carrying the main A3022 road to Brixham on 17th July 1958 with a local service to Kingswear, stands by to hand over the token. Lurking in the background underneath the right hand arch of the road bridge is Hall Class No. 4980 "Wrottesley Hall" in the goods yard, which was situated off the Brixham branch, whilst the front end of a third locomotive is visible on the left awaiting clearance of the road to Paignton and beyond. The bay platform for the Brixham branch train can be seen on the far right. *ASD80-4*

Opposite Bottom: On the same day the Brixham auto, headed by Newton Abbot based Class 1400 0-4-2T No. 1466, occupies its dedicated bay platform at Churston awaiting its next departure. One coach was usually quite sufficient for the reduced loads being experienced at the start of the 1960s and indeed it was to be only another 2½ years before the branch succumbed to complete closure as even the single car DMU which replaced steam in 1961 was unable to save the line. *H1505*

BRIXHAM

Aspect: south-south-east. Altitude: 400 feet. Soil: red loam. Beach: pebble and sand. Water supply: plentiful, soft.

Built on cliffs and hills above its massive harbour, Brixham, as the "Mother" of the Trawling Fishery, is still largely engrossed with its great fishing fleet, but there are new houses and hotels on the gorse-clad cliffs, and a holiday camp above Fishcombe Bay, to testify to its growing popularity as a resort town. A statue of William of Orange on the quay commemorates his landing at Brixham in 1688 on his way to claim the English crown and Berry Head House, where the Rev. H. F. Lyte, first vicar of Lower Brixham, wrote "Abide with me", is now a hotel.

Below: Brixham's terminus suffered from being high above the harbour, in order to restrict gradients between Churston and the town, and following severe cuts in train services, due to a coal strike in 1951, traffic never really recovered, such that a single coach often sufficed for later years. Even the development of holiday camps in the area did little to help the railway as campers were usually bussed from Churston direct to the camps. Here we see Collett 1400 Class No. 1452 at the terminus on 21st August 1958. Railway staff relax on the station seat untroubled by much custom and it is surprising that the passenger service lasted until it did in 1963. *AEB4033*

Opposite Top: The exterior of Brixham's wooden station building seen in this view of 3rd June 1960 dated from the opening of the line in 1868 and was adorned with a canopy to protect passengers from the elements in this rather exposed position. The building on the far right was the gentlemen's convenience which was constructed in brick. The car parked outside the building on the left exhibits the unmistakeable "razor back" lines of a Triumph Mayflower whilst one of the posters advertises cheap trips to Dawlish for 3/10 (19p). After closure the station site was developed for housing. *H1503*

Below: Also on 3ʳᵈ June 1960, 1400 Class No. 1446 waits at the platform before propelling auto coach No. W224W back to the junction at Churston with the 1:50 pm departure. Journey time for the two mile trip was just 7 minutes and the timetable rather candidly admitted that "A frequent service of Devon General omnibuses operates between Churston Station and Brixham (Bolton Cross)." After the Brixham line closed this particular auto coach went on to service on the Gloucester - Chalford shuttle. Coal still seems to be handled in the goods yard seen on the right although of course often coal merchants continued to use railway goods yards even when coal was no longer delivered by rail. *H1504*

KINGSWEAR FOR DARTMOUTH
Early closing: Wednesday

Kingswear, which faces Dartmouth across the beautiful estuary of the Dart, is completely modern, although there are the ruins of a castle on the shore, contemporary with that of Dartmouth. Kingswear's houses are terraced nearly to the summit of a wooded hill, and there is a charming tree shaded walk to the coast, and a frequent ferry service to Dartmouth.

Above: The large running in board left passengers in no doubt that they had reached the end of the line whilst, waiting with a local service to Newton Abbot on 21st August 1958, is the ubiquitous No. 4117. The houses in the background are situated on the hillside on the far bank of the River Dart and today command a premium in the property hotspot of Dartmouth. The wooden overall roof of the station can also be seen beyond the train's coaches and this delightful feature remains in situ today under the auspices of the Torbay Steam Railway. *AEB4037*

Opposite Top: The proximity of the quay at Kingswear is evident in this view of Taunton based Hall Class No. 4985 "Allesley Hall" with the 1:10 pm service for Newton Abbot, seen against a background of dockside cranes. The dockside sidings seen on the right are today occupied by an area of hard standing for yachts and other craft being refurbished or over wintered. *H1500*

Opposite Bottom: Next to a rake of coal wagons, a local service to Newton Abbot hauled by 5100 Class No. 5196 prepares to get under way on 7th July 1958. In this year, in addition to the three named expresses which had through coaches to Kingswear, namely the "Torbay Express", the "Devonian" and the "Mayflower", Kingswear enjoyed a further fifteen departures on weekdays. No. 5196 did not have much longer in service, being withdrawn at the end of 1959 having worked for twenty-five years. *ASD80-5*

Our final view sees the train on the left emptying its complement of passengers followed by the guard with satchel and billycan. Many will no doubt be making their way to the ferry, whilst at the opposite platform No. 4992 "Crosby Hall" waits with an up service on 2nd September 1958. The "Steam Packet" inn looks down on proceedings as indeed it still does today. *PY10051K*

DARTMOUTH

Altitude: sea level to 600 feet. Beach: pebbles near the castle.
Lovely Dartmouth, of many memories, suns itself beside the emerald Dart in beautiful South Devon. A thousand years and more of stirring history are bound up with Dartmouth, the "cradle of the British Navy". A sea history of breathless adventures by Dartmouth men, whose tradition is carried on by the gay young cadets from the Royal Naval College on the hill above the town. The historic 17th century Butterwalk, unfortunately damaged during an air raid, has now been restored to its rightful place as one of the greatest attractions of Dartmouth.

Right: Full to the gunwales, if not positively overloaded, with holidaymakers, this 1949 view of the paddle steamer "Kingswear Castle" shows the vessel having just cast off from Dartmouth. A rake of coaching stock just visible on the far shore shows the position of the railway to Kingswear which was just a short ferry ride away. Happily "Kingswear Castle" is still delighting tourists today on the Dart estuary, being the UK's only coal fired paddle steamer. She was built in Dartmouth in 1924 and plied regularly between Totnes and Dartmouth until 1966. *SR153*

Below: There are records of a ferry linking Kingswear and Dartmouth as early as 1365. In 1908 a new twin screw ferry named "The Mew", seen in this 1949 view, replaced earlier paddle steamers named "Perseverance" and "Dolphin" on the short crossing. In 1924 she was altered to carry the GWR's road vehicles in order to avoid the heavy payments made for the use of the Lower vehicle ferry. In 1940 she steamed to Dover to take part in the Dunkirk evacuation but was deemed unsuitable for the task and returned to Dartmouth from where she was finally withdrawn on 8 October 1954. *SR154*

KINGSBRIDGE

The Western National run a regular road motor service between Kingsbridge and the seaside resorts of Salcombe, Torcross, Thurlestone, etc. Kingsbridge is set in the fertile district of the South Hams, at the head of the pretty inlet of the Salcombe estuary. There is superb yachting, boating and bathing in the estuary, and the town is the centre for a network of bus services to some of the most famous beauty spots of south west Devon.

Below: A magnificent panorama of the station site at Kingsbridge with 4500 Class No. 5533 at the platform in this undated view as the train crew take it easy on one of the platform seats whilst chatting to a waiting passenger. The yard seems to be reasonably full with wagons, vans and coaching stock including a couple of coal trucks seen by the former locomotive shed, which had closed in September 1961, on the far right of this view. The corrugated iron shelter, seen to the left of the run round loop, provided accommodation for two carriages. By the final year there were just six departures from Kingsbridge on Mondays - Fridays rising to nine, including one containing through carriages to Paddington, on summer Saturdays. *FW15-5 5525*

Opposite Top: On the 9th September 1961 4500 Class tank No. 5525 has charge of the 2:10 pm service from Kingsbridge which continued on to Totnes after calling at the main line junction for the branch at Brent. It had been the original intention to extend the line five miles along the Kingsbridge estuary to Salcombe and, given the popularity of the latter destination today, this may well have enabled the branch to survive beyond its closure in 1963. As it was, a bus connection had to suffice from Kingsbridge, details of which, operated by the Western National Omnibus Co. (heavy luggage not conveyed), were shown in the BR timetable. *FW15-3*

Opposite Bottom: The ground signal is "off" as Newton Abbot based No. 5573 prepares to run round having just brought in a service from Brent on 3rd June 1960. The attractive stone built station building lasted for some 46 years after closure before finally succumbing to demolition in 2009. Behind the running in board the advertisements proclaim that "Brylcreem puts life into dry hair" and passengers are invited to book their accommodation at the Cottage Hotel at Hope Cove which is still trading today. *H1490*

PLYMOUTH

Population 250,000. Market days: Tuesdays, Thursdays and Saturdays. Subsoil: limestone and shale
Plymouth, one of the most devastatingly bombed places in England, has been one of the first to
publish a comprehensive and admirable plan for rebuilding. There is an important Marine Biological
Station at Plymouth and the seawater swimming pool and colonnade walk and sun terraces are
intact. Devonport is now a part of the city of Plymouth.

Below: The up Penzance – Wolverhampton service, better known as "The Cornishman", is seen at
Plymouth's North Road station headed by County Class No. 1006 appropriately named "County of
Cornwall" on 16th May 1954. Although based at Plymouth Laira at this time it would shortly be transferred
to Carmarthen for a five month stay before returning to the West Country, reallocated to Penzance shed.
It was to have a working life of less than 19 years before withdrawal in 1964. Named expresses were
usually grouped together, often on coloured pages, in the WR timetable although the proofreader did not
spot, in the list of calling points for the "Cornishman" in the summer 1963 edition, that it apparently
stopped at "Western-super-mare". Westernisation taken a little too far perhaps! *REV84A*

Opposite Top: North British Warship D602 "Bulldog" in blue livery is seen towards the end of its even
shorter life, just under 10 years, light engine at Plymouth on 4th April 1967. It was withdrawn from Laira
depot, along with the other four class members, at the end of 1967 and scrapped at Cashmore's in
Newport the following year. By this time the design was considered to be non-standard, even for hydraulic
types, and though reliability was reportedly not an issue, due to the fact that BR had been instructed to
reduce the number of main line locomotive classes then operating by nearly 50%, primarily by eliminating
types which were either known to be unreliable, had high maintenance costs or were so few in number as
to be non-standard, they had to go. *ASV68-1D*

Opposite Bottom: A panorama of the layout, with a profusion of ground signals, at the east end of
Plymouth station in this undated view reveals the arrival of Hall Class No. 6938 "Corndean Hall" whilst
Castle Class No. 5078, originally named "Lamphey Castle", but renamed "Beaufort" in 1941, gets under
way with an up service. *REV601/1*

Opposite Top: All signals to stop as the up "Cornishman" is again seen, this time with an unidentified Hall Class at its head carrying reporting number 675. At the adjacent platform County Class No. 1005 "County of Devon" waits with another up service. This view is undated but reporting number 675 was certainly used for this service during the period 1956-58. *REV88C-5*

Opposite Bottom: An interesting view of track renewals being undertaken at Plymouth during April 1961. Although it was not always possible to undertake such work outside the holiday peak periods, the spring would have been a suitable time in terms of minimising traffic disruption. A steam crane and steam hauled ballast train are evident in this view. The new headquarters building, planned mainly to house the Plymouth Divisional office known as Intercity House opened by Dr. Beeching in 1962, is seen rising in the background. This was soon to prove something of a white elephant as it was occupied by fewer and fewer BR staff in a world of constantly changing management structures, the notable railway author G. Freeman Allen describing it as "one of many monuments to perennially changing opinion on how and where to run a British railway". Work started in 2020 to convert the building into a University of Plymouth campus to be known as Intercity Place. The building is to be refurbished inside and out and topped with a ring of LED lighting as part of area regeneration plans. *RCR15681*

Above: On 13th July 1958 Reading based Castle Class No. 5018 "St. Mawes Castle", which is taking over a service from Paddington brought in by King Class No. 6026, is signalled away from Plymouth with a departure for the west. Due to weight restrictions on the Royal Albert Bridge, Kings were banned from working west of Plymouth.

Top: Having brought in the service now taken over by No. 5018 in the previous image, King Class No. 6026 "King John" retires light engine and tender first to its home shed at this time, Laira depot, for servicing. This magnificent locomotive gains some admiring glances from the family walking along the street on the far right. Who would have thought at the time that the Kings were destined to last in service for only another four years.

BARNSTAPLE
Population 15,940. Climate: mild.
Barnstaple, with its many arched bridge across the River Taw, is an ancient town which makes a superb touring centre for north Devon. The modern public parks and gardens enhance the attractions of the town which has stately Georgian houses in the suburb of Newport. The modern boundaries of Barnstaple now include Pilton on the northern side of the River Yeo. John Gay of "Beggar's Opera" fame was born in the town and educated at the town's grammar school.

Bottom: A real period piece this – 3300 Class No. 3444 "Cormorant" is seen at Barnstaple Junction with a service for Taunton. The fireman is raking coal forward ready for the journey and notice that a tablet catcher is fitted to the tender, necessary to speed up transit of the long single line to Taunton. The Bird class were double-framed inside cylinder 4-4-0s, being a development of the Bulldog class with strengthened outside frames. A total of fifteen of these were built with No. 3444 lasting in service until 1951. Although the WR had its own station at Barnstaple, Victoria Road, through services for Ilfracombe were either obliged to reverse at Victoria Road or after 1905 take the avoiding line and call at the SR's two Barnstaple stations of Junction and Town. This view is dated June 1937. *GW223*

Above: 4300 Class No. 6390 positions stock at Barnstaple Junction in this undated view. The lines in the foreground led off to Bideford and Torrington and those diverging to the left to Ilfracombe, with the steps of the signal box situated in the divergence between the two routes, visible on the left. No. 6390 was Taunton based from October 1953 until withdrawal in May 1962. Today just a single track serves a much rationalised Barnstaple. *REV279-2*

Below: On 1st June 1960 No. 6390, having earlier left Ilfracombe with the 3 pm service to Taunton, is seen running round at Victoria Road station. Seven minutes were allowed for this manoeuvre with an allowance of a further 101 minutes for the remaining 44 ¾ miles to Taunton with thirteen intermediate stops. Another fine example of the distinctive Triumph Mayflower adorns the station approach. Victoria Road closed to passengers twelve days after this image was taken but remained open for goods until March 1970. *H1429*

Cornwall

SALTASH

Linked by frequent trains or a half hourly bus and ferry service with the centre of Plymouth, Saltash offers all the joys of a quiet open air holiday with the advantages of a city. Almost incredibly steep streets lead up from the shores of the Tamar estuary to the ancient church and Guildhall and the modern town at the Cornish end of the great Royal Albert Bridge built by Brunel in 1859 to carry the railway over the Tamar. There is bathing, boating and yachting on the estuary and innumerable walks to places of interest in the neighbourhood.

Below: Although lacking a headboard this is the "Cornish Riviera" express which began operating in 1904 and has Castle Class No. 5069 "Isambard Kingdom Brunel" at its head which is perhaps appropriate as it is about to cross the great engineer's magnificent Royal Albert Bridge shortly after passing through Saltash with the up service sometime in 1949. There is a 45 mph speed restriction through the station curves which reduces to just 15 mph on the approaches to the bridge, which of course always has been, and remains today, merely single track. *REV46 B24*

Opposite Top: No mention of Saltash would be complete without featuring the famous Plymouth Auto which provided a frequent train service between Plymouth and Saltash in the days before the competing road bridge was completed in 1961 thereby creaming off much of the local rail traffic. In 1958 for example there were no less than 23 departures of this shuttle service on weekdays from Saltash serving Devonport, St. Budeaux and the dockyards en route to Plymouth. In this view, taken on 13th July 1958, push-pull fitted Collett 64XX Class pannier tank No. 6406 has just arrived from the city. *ASD65-5*

Opposite Bottom: The driver leans well out of his cab to sight signals as Britannia pacific No. 70021 "Morning Star" rounds the curve out of Saltash station with the down "Cornish Riviera" express in April 1952. No. 70021 had been allocated from new to Plymouth's Laira depot the previous August and would stay there until January 1957 when it transferred to Cardiff Canton. Along with many of the Standard types No. 70021 had a short working life, being withdrawn at the end of 1967 from Carlisle Kingmoor depot. *REV65B 4 1*

Observed by two gentlemen from the road above the station, the 3.16pm departure from Saltash starts its crossing of the Tamar in April 1952. This was the noon service from Penzance forming a through train to Glasgow Central which was joined at Plymouth by a portion for Manchester London Road. Glaswegians returning home from Penzance were in for a 19½ hour marathon before reaching the Scottish city at 7:28 am the following morning although there was a helpful note in the timetable advising that passengers could reach Glasgow a whole 40 minutes earlier at 6:48 am by changing at Crewe! *REV65B*

LOOE

Population 3,782. Aspect: south. Subsoil: limestone.

The twin towns of East and West Looe, facing each other across the mouth of the Looe River, offer holidaymakers all the delights of sea and river. Their attractive houses cluster in a friendly huddle on the narrow ledges beside the river or attempt to climb the steep banks to the more modern villas and hotels high on the cliffs of Hannafore Hill. Looe Island, although privately owned, is usually open to visitors on Thursdays.

The attractive riverside location of the original Looe station building is evident in this view, taken on 18th. July 1960, of No. 4559 entering with a service from Liskeard. The grassy area between the track and the large tree bounded by the small saplings once contained stone bordered flower beds spelling out the station name. Quay sidings beyond the original station site were subsequently taken out of use in November 1963 and the line cut back in April 1968 with the local police station now standing where the original station and most of the platform once was. Although this meant that the current station is now less conveniently situated for the town centre, at least the line, which was proposed for closure in the Beeching Report and reprieved just two weeks before closure was due to be implemented in 1966, has survived into the 21st Century. *RCR15105*

Opposite Top: On the 18th July 1960 Class 4500 4MT tank No. 4552 is seen by the rather slender platform mounted water tank and crane refilling its tanks prior to its next journey up the valley to the main line at Liskeard. These prairie tanks, to a Churchward design intended for lightly laid branch lines, were introduced in 1906. Worthy of note is the station totem sign fixed to an adjacent lamppost which would no doubt command a high price in the railwayana market today. *RCR15103*

Opposite Bottom: This undated view of No. 5519 shows the position of the quay sidings which allowed the locomotive to run round its train before returning to the junction, there being only a single line adjacent to the platform with no run round facility at that point. Judging by the piles of sleepers it would appear that some replacement has taken place or is intended in the near future. The seven arch bridge spanning the Looe River seen in the background separates East and West Looe and whilst the river is undoubtedly an asset to the attractiveness of the town it is also something of a double edged sword in that flooding regularly occurs when a high spring tide combines with heavy rainfall leading to a swollen river. Looe is apparently the most frequently flooded coastal town in the UK, with £39m of damage to homes and businesses having been caused during the last five years. The current bridge dates from 1853 having replaced a narrow medieval bridge of fifteen arches. *NS2021150*

Below: This view of a goodly crowd of intending passengers awaiting the next service allows us to examine the neat single platform station building. The one advertisement that can be readily deciphered is for "Snowcem", modestly making the claim that "The effect is dazzling", a brand of masonry paint which is still manufactured today to the original formulation some 60 years on.

FOWEY

Population: 2,500. Plentiful supply of water, slightly hard. Market day: Saturday.
Recreations: tennis, bowls, boating, golf (9 holes),cricket, bathing, yachting and fishing.
Fowey is a fascinating example of the Cornish genius for utilising a difficult site to create a town of uncommon charm. Its narrow streets and flights of steps defy the most persistent chars-a-banc drivers but it has a charm all its own for those who explore its odd byways and many ancient buildings. Fowey is the "Troy Town" of the novels of the late Sir Arthur Quiller-Couch, writing as "Q", and the neighbourhood has also been described in Daphne du Maurier's fiction. "Q" writes of Fowey thus - "The visitor, if he be at all of my mind, will find a charm in Fowey over and above its natural beauty and what I may call its holiday conveniences, for the yachtsman, for the sea fisherman, or for one content to idle in peaceful waters. It has a flourishing trade and a life of its own which I am happy to say keepeth wholly unlike the ordinary seaside resort with its "season" and long blank interval of hungering for lodgers".

Above: Class 1400 tanks were often to be seen on the picturesque Fowey branch and this example, No. 1419, was captured at the platform at journey's end on 31st May 1960. Indeed, this branch line was the only example in the county which regularly played host to these diminutive 0-4-2 tank locomotives with No. 1419 being the regular locomotive. Of particular interest in this view is the clerestory vehicle parked in the bay which acted as a staff coach. *H1402*

Below: Illustrating the importance of the china clay traffic to the line is this view of Warship D816 "Eclipse", then just 5 months old, hauling a rake of empty clay wagons on the goods avoiding line whilst Collett 1400 tank No. 1419, standing clear of the running lines, occupies the bay platform on 22nd July 1960 prior to its next journey. The following year the passenger service would be dieselised and No. 1419 would be withdrawn from service at nearby St. Blazey shed in April 1961. *RCR15186*

PAR
Beach: sand. Early closing: Thursday.

Par station serves the three villages of Par, St. Blazey and Tywardreath, all within sight and easy reach of each other. Par, set beside the splendid sands of St. Austell bay, has a harbour well known to yachtsmen and is important as an outlet for the china-clay traffic.

Top: At an unrecorded date in 1960 County Class No. 1008 "County of Cardigan" enters Par with a service to Penzance. The rather massive station running in board leaves the passenger in no doubt that this is the junction for Newquay and the station for the nearby Carlyon Bay Hotel. *NS201046*

Bottom: The Newquay branch service stands ready at the bay platform with 4500 Class No. 4569 at its head on 9th July 1955. *RCR6359*

PENRYN

The 13th century Glasney College, slight traces of which still remain, made Penryn a centre of Cornish literature, and the town is still a busy place with a Georgian town hall and other Regency buildings. Set at the head of the Penryn River, a tributary of the Fal, it is within easy reach of Falmouth, Truro and the Lizard peninsula.

From the vantage point of the signal box, seemingly a young child rather than the Penryn signalman keeps a close eye on the token exchange undertaken by the fireman of Hawksworth 9400 Class pannier tank No. 9476 on 15th August 1959 as it enters the station from Truro. The signal box dates from the 1923 remodelling of the station and is unusual in having a rendered, rather than an exposed brick or stone, base and weather boarded upper level. The box contained 32 levers and remained in service until November 1971. *PH000306*

FALMOUTH
Population 15,500. Climate: mild and balmy.

One of the largest towns in Cornwall, Falmouth has a glorious setting on the wide estuary of the River Fal, and has one of the finest and most capacious harbours in Great Britain, which sheltered many invasion barges, waiting for "D Day", during the war. Before the war the Royal Cornwall Yacht Club, with the clubs of Flushing and St. Mawes, provided races throughout the year. Such enterprising clubs will doubtless get going again as soon as possible.

4500 Class No. 5546 rests at the terminus of Falmouth Docks in 1959 with its two coach train whilst the crew take the opportunity to relax on one of the station seats situated in front of the fencing supporting an enamel sign, now undoubtedly a collectors' piece, advertising the famous Camp coffee. This product, created in 1885 by R. Paterson & Son of Glasgow, consisted of a concentrated syrup flavoured with coffee and chicory. The advertising image on the bottle's label gave rise to the legend that it was originally created as an instant coffee for military use, showing as it does a seated Gordon Highlander being served by a Sikh soldier holding a tray with a bottle of essence and jug of hot water. *NS201227B*

Below: On 30th May 1960 Manor Class No. 7813 "Freshford Manor" is shunting empty carriage stock at the terminus. The locomotive was based at Truro (83F) shed at this time and was possibly filling in on a turn on the branch which would normally be undertaken by nothing more powerful than a tank locomotive. However there were through coaches from Falmouth to Paddington which joined a train from Penzance at Truro, so larger locomotives such as Manors were provided for these services. *LRF4631*

Opposite Top: This exterior view of a trio of passengers leaving the station reveals its proximity to the docks as evidenced by the tall cranes seen in the background. Camping coach W9929W which was an ex Churchward TK coach numbered 3634, which was itself rebuilt from an earlier World War I ambulance coach, occupies a bay on the left whilst just peeping out from the right of the station is the nose of a BR lorry used for local deliveries. Camping coaches were located at Penryn and Perranwell on the Falmouth branch at various times. The attractive station building, which contained the usual provision of ticket office, gentlemens' toilets, ladies' waiting room and toilets and a general waiting room, sadly succumbed to demolition about 1969. *W2229W*

Opposite Bottom: DMUs in the shape of three single car units have arrived on the Falmouth branch as this view taken on 11th July 1961 reveals although steam is obviously still present as witnessed by the smoke in the station area in the background. Steam infrastructure in the shape of the water tank and crane seen on the left is also still evident. *RCR16073*

HAYLE

Early closing: Thursday

The great Cornish cliffs sink to sandy towans in the Hayle estuary, where there is splendid bathing and boating. Although primarily a manufacturing town, Hayle is also a good centre for picnicking and camping. There is a ferry across the mouth of the estuary which brings Lelant within a short walk.

Above: A delightful panorama of the railway in Hayle featuring Grange Class No. 6832 "Brockton Grange" which has just left Hayle station, seen on the far right, and begins its crossing of the 831 foot viaduct, consisting of 36 masonry piers with longitudinal riveted plate girders supporting transverse timber decking, on 14th August 1959 with a service for Penzance. The site of the former Hayle Railway terminus which was demolished in 1948 lay in front of the viaduct. A couple of Morris Minors together with an Austin of even greater vintage enhance the relatively traffic free scene, on what was at that time the main A30, whilst a couple of intending passengers wait at the bus stop positioned outside the local branch of Lloyds bank in Foundry Square which remarkably is still in operation today. One of the few changes in the modern scene, apart from the increase in traffic, is the removal of the bus stop outside the bank to its new position around the corner outside the Post Office. *PH000505*

Below: Seen from the station footbridge, Hall Class No. 4905 "Barton Hall", a Newton Abbot based locomotive since June 1956, runs over the viaduct and into Hayle station with a Penzance service. Semaphore signalling and a platform end water crane complete this 1959 view. The track leading off to the right led down to Hayle wharves on a gradient of 1 in 30. *PH000228*

MARAZION
Early Closing: Wednesday

Marazion on Mount's Bay has many attractions for a quiet family holiday but its chief glory is St. Michael's Mount, reached at low tide by a causeway.

St Michael's Mount featured on one of the bookmarks given away with "Holiday Haunts". The other bookmarks in the series featured Devil's Bridge, Gloucester Cathedral, Tintern Abbey, The Vale of Llangollen and Warwick Castle.

Hawksworth County Class No. 1002 "County of Berks" gathers speed as it passes through Marazion nonstop with an up service in 1959. Passenger services were withdrawn from here in October 1964 and this is now one of seventeen closed stations on the Cornish main line between Plymouth and Penzance.
PH000223

PENZANCE
Subsoil: clay and gravel. Beach: sand and shingle. Climate: mild.

Penzance has many claims upon the interest and affection of its visitors. It has had a long history and is the terminal for the Cornish Riviera Express, one of the most famous trains in the world. Its climate is so equable that it is bowered in flowers all through the year. Although of ancient origin Penzance has suffered from Spanish raiders and Parliamentarian soldiers to such an extent that its earliest buildings are of the Georgian period. Not only is Penzance the centre of a great flower growing district famous for its early daffodils and other spring flowers but it has in the Morrab and other gardens a collection of sub tropical trees and flowers growing to perfection in the open air.

Below: Castle Class No. 4089 "Donnington Castle", wearing light green livery and named after a castle two miles north of Newbury, is captured at Penzance terminus in September 1949. It was constructed in July 1925 and withdrawn nearly 40 years later in January 1965. *MC20378*

Opposite Top: An unrecorded 1940s view of Penzance reveals Manor Class No. 7812 "Erlestoke Manor" at the head of a service whose carriage boards cannot be deciphered at this distance. The platform mounted signals on the right have banner repeaters in addition to the more usual semaphore arms. No. 7812 is fortunately still with us, having been preserved at the Severn Valley Railway where two classmates are also part of the locomotive stable. *MC20363*

Opposite Bottom: In a similar position to the previous image but photographed from Chyandour Road, high up on the other side of the station sometime during the 1950s, is Hall Class No. 7905 "Fowey Hall". The proximity of the station to the sea is very evident in this view and the importance of milk traffic to the railways at that time is borne out by the impressive collection of churns on the platform. The tall tower of St. Mary's church dominates the skyline and a church has stood on this headland since the 12th Century. The present building dates from 1835 with the tower acting as a landmark for the local sea faring community. *MC1005P*

Above: The diesel hydraulic era is very much in evidence with four examples of locomotives apparent in this 9th April 1960 panorama of the station area. On display is a pair of North British Class 22 "Baby Warships", Nos. D6314 and D6306, with an unidentified Warship at the adjacent platform, whilst signalled away on the right is classmate D814 "Dragon" which had only entered service 3 months prior to this view. A lone railwayman walks up the "four foot" with billycan in hand either ready for his next shift or on his way home after completing his duty. *RCR14618*

Opposite: Our final view of Penzance illustrates the interior of the station sheltering underneath the protection of

the overall roof. This structure dated from the GWR's redevelopment of the station in 1876 and was 250 feet long by 80 feet wide. The roof was refurbished in 2012/13. Just arrived is a pair of North British Type 2s, D6304 coupled in front of the doyen of the class, D6300, on 30th May 1960 with the 9:10 am service from Plymouth which, if on schedule, should make the time 11:50 am. *LRF4641*

LELANT
Golf (18 holes).
Lelant, within 3 miles of St. Ives, has one of the most famous golf courses in Cornwall laid out on the sand dunes above the Hayle estuary and giving magnificent views of the cliff bound coast beyond. A ferry below links the ancient church of St. Uny Lelant and the village with Hayle and Godrevy Head.

Above: Looking in the direction of St. Ives, a branch service from the Cornish tourist honeypot has just arrived on an unrecorded date in 1959 with No. 4566 running bunker first in charge. The original station building was of wooden construction presumably because of problems in providing adequate foundations for a stone structure so close to the riverbank. It was later subsumed sympathetically into a dwelling which stands to this day and as an added bonus serves cream teas in the season. *PH000210*

Below: The picturesque waterside setting of Lelant station on the St. Ives branch line by the estuary of the River Hayle is evident in this view of 4500 Class prairie tank No. 4570 entering the station on 30th May 1960. Staffing had ceased 18 months prior to this date and at one time a branch had led down to the small quay located nearby. These days Lelant boasts another station at Lelant Saltings which acts as a park and ride facility to ease problems in traffic choked St. Ives.

CARBIS BAY

Aspect: North. Altitude: 300 feet. Subsoil: granite. Beach: sand. Climate: mild, yet bracing. Churches: CofE and Methodist.

Early closing: Thursday.
The beautiful, well sheltered, Carbis Bay, with its wooded chine and great stretch of sands, has a small colony of fine houses, hotels and bungalows for permanent residence or a quiet holiday. A frequent service of buses link it with St. Ives.

Above: In those tranquil days before the G7 summit descended upon the community and raised its worldwide profile, Carbis Bay witnesses the departure of No. 4570 for St.Ives on 30th May 1960. The continuing popularity of the railway here is evidenced by the fact that passenger numbers for each of the three years 2017/18 – 2019/20 have topped 200,000 annually. As can be seen the line is situated in a shallow cutting north of the road that leads down to the beach. *H1355*

Right: Seen from the bridge which crosses the line, and looking towards St. Ives, the steepness of the cutting sides can be seen and as a consequence of the restricted space at platform level the main station building, seen on the left, was situated at road level. *LRF4671*

ST. IVES
Subsoil: blue elvin. Beaches: beautiful sand. Excellent water supply.

St. Ives is such a mellow lovable place with its white houses basking in the sunshine that there is little wonder that it has a permanent colony of artists who are quick to defend the quaint and picturesque byways of the older town from any encroachments. Among the famous painters who have lived there in the past are Whistler, Richard Sickert, and Anders Zorn, the Swedish painter and etcher, whose picture of "Evening at St. Ives" was bought by the Luxembourg Gallery in Paris. It takes its name from St. Ia who built a monastery in the 5th century on what is now called The Island.

And so we come to St. Ives, beloved of the artistic community and tourists alike, as No. 4563 runs in and the footplate crew prepare to hand over the single line token to the shirt-sleeved signalman. The station was perched on the side of the hill with spectacular views which no doubt filled the trains of excited holidaymakers with anticipation of a great stay. The prairie tank will shortly stable the carriage stock, run round and subsequently couple up ahead of sister locomotive No. 4570 to form the 5:15 pm departure for St. Erth on 30th May 1960. *H1359*

Above: A year earlier in 1959 the crew of No. 4566 take the opportunity to chat to the signalman with token in hand before departing for the main line. The occupants of the Camp Coach seen parked on the left have taken the chance to dry some washing on a line strung from the carriage door. If you did not mind the proximity of the station this must have been an idyllic spot in which to spend a week's holiday which for a few pounds a week, plus at least six rail tickets from your home to the destination, constituted a relatively inexpensive holiday. In 1952, for example, a week off season (March and October) would have cost £7 whilst in July and August the charge rose to £10. *NS201172A*

Below: Its passengers having alighted, including some schoolgirls with the obligatory satchels and dressed in the demure fashions of the day with skirts well below the knee – as distinct from today's style – No. 4570 runs round prior to returning with No. 4566 as described above. The special occasion giving rise to the bunting hung about the station was not recorded by the photographer.

PERRANPORTH

Beach: three miles of soft sand. Climate: bracing, equable. Churches: CofE, R.C., Methodist.

Perranporth, on the north coast, was a secluded village not so long ago, but it is now developing as a small but enterprising family resort. It has impressive cliffs and an enormous stretch of pale gold sand where the long Atlantic rollers make surf-bathing a thrilling sport. The curious little "lost" church of St. Piran is nearby.

Above: The island platform of Perranporth plays host to No. 4593 on an unrecorded date in 1960. The contents of the guard's compartment are being unloaded onto a trolley during the station stop and fire buckets hang from their hooks on the end wall which also houses a fire extinguisher in its cupboard. Just a quarter of a mile away was the town's second station – the halt at Perranporth Beach, two minutes being allowed in the timetable to travel this distance. At this time No. 4593, along with other motive power used on the branch, was allocated to Truro depot. *NS201049*

Opposite Top: At the Newquay end of the station the signalman returns to his box whilst the crew of No. 5557 while away the time, no doubt waiting to cross with another service on this single track route. A subway gave access to the island platform, the site of which is now occupied by an industrial estate built in the 1970s. *H1371*

Opposite Bottom: This view taken from the carriage of a Newquay bound train entering the station illustrates the crossing of services at Perranporth, the most important traffic centre on the route. The small goods yard provided here is on the right and dealt mainly with coal but, as the whole route ran through relatively unproductive agricultural districts apart from Perranporth and sporadic Treamble branch mineral output, goods traffic on the line was generally insignificant. *PY1003P*

ST. AGNES

Early Closing: Wednesday.
St. Agnes is a far larger place than it seems at first sight. A wooded valley half a mile long leads down to the sandy beach of Trevannance and the famous landmark of St. Agnes beacon is a mile away. Within a mile and a half along the coast are Chapel Porth and Porthtowan where small clusters of modern houses and bungalows overlook sandy bathing beaches.

Below: No. 4552 runs into St. Agnes sometime in 1959 with a service for Newquay passing the goods shed and yard which again handled mainly coal traffic. Originally constructed on opening of the line in 1903 with a single platform, the station had been rebuilt with the island platform arrangement seen here together with a new 30 lever signal box in 1937 thus allowing trains to pass. 4500 tank locomotives were the general motive power seen on the line although pannier tanks could sometimes deputise. *PH000217*

Opposite Top: As a passenger supervises the loading of an item into the guard's compartment it is apparent that railway staff outnumber passengers by three to one in this view of No. 5557 at the station with a train for Newquay on 30th May 1960. The original building is seen to the right of the running in board and following redesign of the station in 1937 the old platform was demolished and some of the doors and windows of the station building were blanked off. The building survives to the present time as a craft centre. *H1368*

Opposite Bottom: A charming family group, possibly based in the Camp Coach (W9931W) parked in the loading dock, await the next train for Newquay sometime in the 1950s. From 1952-56 St. Agnes had one such coach but this increased to two in the period 1957-61 and ultimately to three in 1962. W9931W had been built in 1910 and converted to a Camp Coach in 1954. The footbridge seen in the background, which connected the station approach to the island platform, was demolished, it is believed, in the late 1950s for it is absent in the previous image and passengers then had to make use of the board crossing to access the platform. *REV69B 2 1*

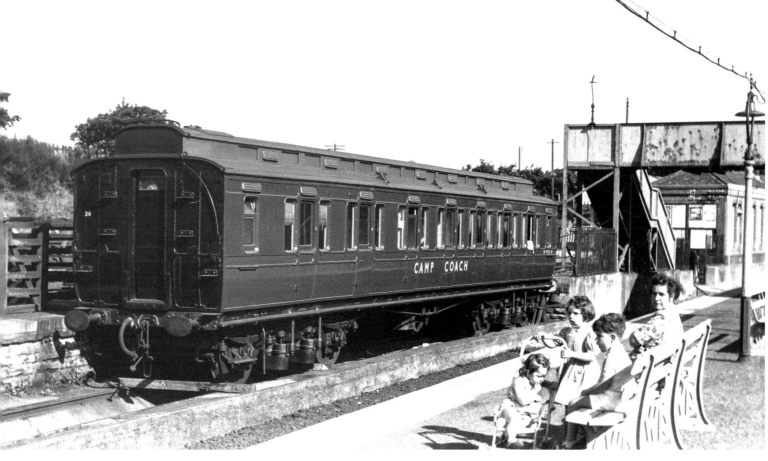

NEWQUAY

Population: 11,500. Altitude: sea level to 300 feet. Plentiful supply of soft water. Subsoil: slate rock.

Newquay is set almost exactly in the centre of the north west coast of Cornwall, on 300 foot cliffs overlooking five sandy bays, so huge they never become overcrowded, even in the height of the season. Newquay is the largest of the North Cornwall resorts and devotes itself wholeheartedly to organising sports, excursions and amusements for its visitors. The older part of the town catches all the tonic sea breezes, but for those who prefer a rather milder climate there is a newer district spreading on the slopes of the Trenance valley, which is sheltered to the north and open to the south. Newquay is one of the chief centres in Cornwall for surf riders and is also a happy hunting ground for the naturalist who can find many rare birds and plants in the neighbourhood.

Below: Newquay, the premier resort of the North Cornwall coast and served by two routes, was an impressive three platform terminus. Our first view, dating from 1960, shows 5100 Class No. 4167 about to depart for Par bunker first. The large building adjacent to the platform was part of Newquay gasworks which ceased production in 1958. Today merely a single running line terminating at a truncated platform serves the resort. *NS201147*

Opposite Top: The 9:15 am from Chacewater has just arrived, hopefully on time exactly an hour later, with a sprinkling of passengers on 31st May 1960 headed by No. 5557. There were some eight or nine departures each way on weekdays on this route with some services being extended to or from Falmouth, after reversal at Truro, on Sundays. *LRF4696*

Opposite Bottom: Departure time for the 10:40 am service to Par is fast approaching according to the station clock as No. 5557 makes ready to leave. This locomotive had brought in a previous service from Chacewater twenty-five minutes earlier as illustrated above. *LRF4699*

Larger motive power was also to be seen at Newquay on some of the through holiday trains as evidenced here in 1959 by Hall Class No.6931 "Aldborough Hall". A young lad is seemingly having something on the tender explained to him by one of the footplate crew.
NS201147A

Somerset

MINEHEAD
Altitude: rising from sea level to 850 feet. Beach: firm sand and shingle.
Recreations: sea and river fishing, theatre, cinema, promenade entertainments, seasonal orchestra.

Sheltered by pine clad North Hill, Minehead has grown from an ancient fishing village to the largest resort of West Somerset, without losing any of its quaint charm. There are fishermen's cottages in Quay Town and rose-bowered thatched cottages on both sides of the steps which lead up to the noble parish church. Minehead has an Assembly Room containing a concert hall, a ballroom and an arcade, and there is also an up to date cinema and a large open air seawater swimming pool. The splendid sands and safe bathing make the town popular as a family resort and it is also celebrated among sportsmen as a centre for stag, fox, hare and otter hunting and for sea and river fishing.

5700 Class pannier tank No. 8745 makes ready for the third departure of the morning from Minehead, the 10:50 am service for Taunton on 24th March 1961. The platform seat seen on the left has the WR of the GWR monogram picked out in white paint as was often the practice with such station furniture following nationalisation in 1948. This 0-6-0PT was a Yeovil based locomotive so had presumably worked up to Taunton and out to Minehead earlier in the day. *FW 7-4 8745*

Above: Back in steam days, on 1st September 1959 to be exact, large prairie tank No. 4128, with "pep pipe" dangling from the cab, heads the next departure for Taunton whilst Collett 2200 Class 0-6-0 No. 2250 shunts the goods yard. The brooding presence of "pine clad North Hill", as Holiday Haunts describes it, is the dramatic backdrop to this scene. *PY10012M*

Below: The new order of diesel power is illustrated by this cross country set rather dwarfed at the long platform, ideal for the lengthy through holiday trains but not really necessary for the local services, seen on 7th September 1968. A considerable number of passengers make their way out of the station possibly heading for the double deck bus waiting outside to take them the short distance to Butlin's holiday camp, which had opened here in 1962. The branch would only have another three years to run under BR ownership but has, of course, fortunately been saved by the preservationists for us to enjoy today. Rationalisation of trackwork has taken place and much of the old goods yard on the right is now devoid of rails, all part of the plan to cut costs and operate a "basic railway". *FWG1181*

WATCHET

Tennis courts and bowling green near the station. Golf course (9 holes) on Cleeve Hill overlooking the sea.

Although Watchet has not the immediate appeal of such places as Selworthy, its quaint charm has an equally enduring quality for those who learn to know it well. It is a glorious playground for children who find endless amusement amongst the rocks and pools which strew the beach and it has two small sandy bays to cater for bathers. Walks in the neighbourhood provide an endless source of pleasure whilst haunts for picnics are to be found in every cleft of the wooded cliffs.

On an unrecorded date in 1955 the station at Watchet witnesses the departure of a service for Minehead hauled by 4500 Class No. 5522. This Taunton based locomotive would remain in service until March 1959. The station building to the right of the footbridge occupies a very restricted site on a sharp bend in South Road, the B3191 from Williton to Carhampton, which carries a great deal more traffic today than was apparent in this view of more than 65 years ago. *NS201018*

WESTON-SUPER-MARE

Beach: sand generally, pebbles at north end. Unlimited supply of pure water. Although Weston-super-Mare suffered severely in air raids, the extensive damage had little effect on its holiday amusements and amenities and no resort has been quicker to return to the gay pleasure round of a peacetime holiday centre. It is a place of more individuality and charm than might be supposed from its claim to be the largest seaside resort between Lancashire and Land's End. Weston's favourite slogan "Air like Wine" is no idle boast. The progressive Weston Corporation, before the War, undertook many schemes for beautifying the town which have more than justified the enormous expense incurred. The Knightstone Medical Baths provide hot seawater, seaweed and foam baths for rheumatic treatment. There is an open air filtered seawater bath to accommodate 1,400 bathers and 5,000 spectators.

Below: Due to the volume of holiday traffic, dedicated excursion platforms were sometimes deemed necessary to cater for this, examples being Southport Chapel Street and Bridlington. In some cases the decision was taken to provide a completely separate excursion station such as happened at Scarborough where the original excursion platforms were replaced with Washbeck excursion station which was renamed Londesborough Road in 1933. Weston-super-mare was originally the terminus of a branch line from the Bristol & Exeter main line which opened in June 1841. The construction of a loop line in 1884 led to Weston gaining a further station on the loop with the original terminus being rebuilt in 1907 and enlarged to four platforms in 1914, known as Locking Road. In this undated view Castle Class No. 5076 "Gladiator" is leaving Locking Road, the Z76 reporting number indicating a special working within the WR or an internal WR excursion. As can be seen a considerable number of sidings were provided to cater for coaching stock together with a turntable and servicing facilities. The tracks on the left led round to the main station in Weston. *MC20566*

Opposite Top: On 2nd September 1955 the station pilot at Locking Road, whose large running in board is prominent in the background, was No. 4595 carrying an 82A Bristol Bath Road shedcode and seen here shunting some motley looking coaching stock, often to be found pressed into service on holiday extras, in one of the numerous carriage sidings. After lying derelict for a number of years, a Tesco store and car park now occupies the site of the station. *ES3099*

Opposite Bottom: Although 40,000 passengers had in the past been handled at Locking Road on bank holiday Mondays, by the early 1960s a sharp downturn in excursion traffic was experienced and the decision was taken to close the excursion station at the end of the 1964 holiday season. In this undated view Modified Hall Class No. 7908 "Henshall Hall" has just arrived at Locking Road with another lengthy excursion train carrying reporting number Z77. This was a Tyseley based locomotive from 1955 until condemnation ten years later. *MS20482*

Above: The main station in Weston, termed Weston-Super-Mare General to distinguish it from the excursion station, is seen in this view of an engineers' train of the late 1950s headed by 9400 Class pannier tank No. 8492 passing through en route to the main line at Uphill Junction. The severe curves of the station platforms, which are protected by glazed canopies, are evident and the middle track is occupied by coaching stock awaiting its next turn. Following the singling of the loop line in 1972 the two signal boxes, one at each end of the station, were closed including the one seen here designated West at the end of the up platform. *WS339*

Below: No mention of Weston would be complete without acknowledging the third station in the town, namely that of the Weston, Clevedon & Portishead Railway (WC&PR) which, although not part of BR, does have a link with the GWR in that the company purchased the railway, but not the land, after closure in 1940 in order to store wagons. The locomotive seen here at the rather basic Weston terminus of Ashcombe Road, Stroudley Terrier No. 2 "Portishead" dating from 1877, was bought by the GWR, painted in GWR livery, and renumbered No. 5 while retaining its name. Initially allocated to St Philip's Marsh depot for shunting and harbour duties, it later saw use at Portishead power station. Surviving into the BR era it then found employment in Bridgwater docks. After a brief sojourn at Newton Abbot as shed pilot it was then put into store at Swindon following which it was broken up in March 1954. Prior to running round its four coach train, one of the locomotive crew is seen trimming the coal in the bunker. *GW275*

CLEVEDON
Population: 9,982. Subsoil: clay and rock. Beach: shingle.

Clevedon grew up around Clevedon Court, the beautiful old manor house built in the reign of Edward II, and although it has spread seaward and developed into a popular holiday resort it has never forgotten its ancient simplicity. Built over seven wooded hills and around three delightful bays it has both charm and individuality. The cottage where Coleridge spent his early married life and where his son Hartley was born is carefully preserved. Clevedon is fully alive to the need for amusements and provides ample facilities for all modern sports in addition to band and orchestral concerts, flannel dances and cinema. (NB A flannel dance apparently just meant that formal evening wear was not required – a forerunner of smart casual perhaps?)

CLEVEDON
THE GEM OF
SUNNY
SOMERSET

A charming natural resort on the Bristol Channel with rocky coast and pebble beaches, and gorgeous sunsets. Steamer trips from the Pier to South Wales resorts and Ilfracombe. Rail and 'bus facilities to Mendips, Bath and lovely Somerset country. Bathing, tennis (hard and grass), putting, bowling greens, golf (18 holes), motor boats. Rowing and paddle boats on Marine Lake. Beautiful walks on cliffs and woods.

Mild climate suitable for Winter visitors who are well catered for.

Official Guide from—PUBLIC RELATIONS OFFICER,
THE COUNCIL HOUSE, CLEVEDON, SOMERSET.

As its name implies, Clevedon was also served by the WC&PR and this view of the other Terrier on the line, the unnamed No. 4, is seen leaving Clevedon station with a coach and wagon during 1940, the last year of operation. Unlike Weston the WC&PR station at Clevedon was adjacent to the GWR station, thereby assisting interchange of goods and passengers. The ex LB&SCR Terrier originally named "Ashstead" and known as No. 4 on the WC&PR was also purchased by the GWR after closure but scrapped eight years later in 1948 but not before it had been involved in lifting the track on the route in 1943. *NS208808*

The attractive exterior of the other station in Clevedon, seen in this view dated 4th July 1959, reveals the proximity of the former WC&PR route which passed between the gap in the buildings apparent to the left of the two cars seen in the background. Sadly this fine building, which was built in 1890 replacing the original timber station of 1847, was demolished in 1968 after closure of the Clevedon branch in October 1966. *H817*

Above: The GWR station boasted a small overall roof, part of the original station that was retained upon rebuilding, which provided some shelter for this pair of autocoaches seen parked at the single platform on 24th May 1953 whilst their locomotive, Collett Class 1400 No. 1430, was undertaking some shunting in the small goods yard. The fine water tower supported by six metal columns adds to the attractiveness of the scene so typical of small country termini throughout the WR. *RCR3876*

Below: Moving on four years to 19th August 1957, prairie tank No. 5565 is captured running round its train prior to a return to the main line junction at Yatton whilst the train guard chats to one of the passengers. At this period, with a journey time of just seven minutes, nearly thirty return journeys were timetabled on the branch on weekdays providing an excellent service attractive to commuters, shoppers and tourists alike. The swan neck gas lamp, seen between the two young lads who are no doubt intrigued at the manoeuvres required to get the locomotive to the front of its train, is a notable adornment to the platform furniture. *PY10159C*

Above: By 10th September 1959 the motive power had changed to this more modern Ivatt tank No. 41249, seen at the terminus as a porter loads the guard's compartment of the single coach with parcels forming the next departure for Yatton. Although such traffic helped to boost the branch's balance sheet, unfortunately it was included in the Beeching Report for closure which duly came in October 1966. *B000241*

Below: The final flowering of motive power used on the branch following dieselisation in August 1960 was this DMU "Bubble car" No. W555013W, sporting "speed whiskers", seen at Clevedon on 2nd August 1965, the year before closure. The driver walks along the platform with lamp in hand ready to attach to the rear of the unit for the return journey. This single car, built by the Gloucester Railway Carriage & Wagon Co. in 1958, had arrived at Bristol Bath Road depot in May 1964 and would depart for Ayr four years later. The overall roof appears to have lost many of its roof tiles by this date and indeed redundant track had been removed and the remaining single line shortened in November 1964 to terminate outside the area covered by the roof following the introduction of DMUs which did not require runround facilities. *AS S93 -1*

PORTISHEAD

Early closing: Thursday.

Portishead is the natural starting point for a tour of the North Somerset coast and a centre for the charming but little known Gordano country whose curious name dates back to the 13th century. It is a countryside of smiling pasture lands and shady woods with prosperous farms and ancient manor houses and Portishead has an atmosphere which blends perfectly with its pastoral charm. Its proximity to Bristol has ensured Portishead's development as a residential centre and it is also becoming increasingly popular as a holiday resort. There is a recreation ground near the Esplanade and a Marine Lake with a splendid corner for children.

With the bulk of the coal fired Portishead power station built in the 1920s looming in the background, this is the old GWR station in the town which, due to expansion of the power station site, was to be replaced by new facilities nearer the town centre in 1954. This view taken from the station footbridge reveals No. 5547 with a service waiting to leave for Bristol and was taken on an unrecorded date in 1950. A venerable lorry with a GWR tarpaulin can be seen waiting outside whilst enamel "Virol" advertising is prominent attached to the platform fencing. For those who didn't have to endure ministrations of this substance, I should explain that it was a brand of malt extract preparation that also included bone marrow and was designed as a nutritional supplement for infants. *NS201138*

Opposite Top: The impressive frontage of the new 1954 station, seen soon after opening on 20th September, was intended to be a modernist statement of investment in the future of railways. However, these hopes were to be short lived for after just 10 years' life it was closed on 7th September 1964 when passenger services ceased on the line to Bristol although freight continued until the early 1980s. At the time it was judged to be a wanton waste of resources and rightly judged to be something of a "white elephant" in the town. Today there is much discussion about bringing back a rail service to Portishead, primarily for commuters, with the traffic choked routes into Bristol no doubt benefiting from such provision. *20.9.54*

Opposite Bottom: At the platform end of the new station on 13th April 1958, where steam age infrastructure of water tank, water cranes and "fire devil" sit uneasily alongside colour light signals, signage and, in the distance, a modern signal box, a prairie tank enters the terminus light engine. The lavish provision of lengthy platforms at the new station tended to dwarf the usual 3 coach steam services and later DMUs operating on the branch. The signal box, which contained 83 levers, remained in use until April 1965 when it too closed just a few months after the station. *PY10071P*

Above: From the lavish to the distinctly basic – this view of the WC&PR facilities at Portishead dates from 1940 and shows railcar No. 5 at the terminus. This Drewry vehicle, which came secondhand from the SR who had tested it on a number of branch lines but found it too small for their purposes, originally had a 50 hp petrol engine but before purchase by the WC&PR this had been replaced by a Parsons 64 hp diesel. There were five rows of 2 x 2 seats with a central gangway for 20 passengers and a transverse bench seat seating six behind the driver's partition, seats being upholstered in green patterned cloth. With a 3 speed gearbox it could obtain a heady 25 mph on a good day with a fair wind. After line closure it was moved to Swindon but ended its days as a pavilion at a local girl's school. *NS208809*

Gloucestershire

SEVERN BEACH

Although this "resort" does not feature in the 1947 guide it had a special place in the hearts of many Bristolians and locals who flocked to this rather unprepossessing spot on the Bristol Channel to sample the attractions on offer, many of which originated from the 1920s. There was a swimming pool called the "Blue Lagoon", a boating lake, dozens of fun-fair stalls, donkey rides operating on grass in the absence of any sandy beach. There was even a cinema which was a corrugated iron building known locally as the "Galvanised Gaumont" whilst Miller's Field provided rather basic accommodation for visitors in chalets, sheds and old bus bodies. Day trippers from Bristol were also attracted by the fact that it enjoyed more relaxed licensing laws than the city and it even became known as the "Blackpool of the West" which is perhaps rather overstating the case. As its time as a holiday and pleasure resort came to an end in the 1970s many attractions and shops closed and the village pub called the Severn Salmon, which was formerly the Severn Beach Hotel, was demolished to make way for housing. Infilling of the Blue Lagoon took place in the 1980s closely followed by demolition of the station buildings, however the platform and a single track survive, still providing a service into Bristol today.

Below: Bristol based Standard 3MT tank No. 82038, which shuttled between the city's Bath Road, St. Phillip's Marsh and Barrow Road depots between 1960 and withdrawal in 1965, waits to depart bunker first from the bay platform at Severn Beach with the 1:30 pm (Saturdays only) service calling at all stations to Bristol Temple Meads on 17th February 1962. The corner of the main station building, which was set at right angles to the platform facing Station Road, can just be seen in the far left background. Sidings on the right, originally intended for the berthing of excursion train coaching stock, still see some use judging by the wagons parked there but freight services were to be withdrawn the following year.

Opposite Top: A 3 car DMU waits at the through platform at Severn Beach on 16th July 1963. Services beyond the level crossing gates seen behind the DMU to Pilning (Low Level) and thence back to Bristol, thus completing a circular route from the city, were to cease in November the following year although freight continued to use this route until 1968. This image gives a closer view of the 1924 station concourse building which was fronted by a large canopy, the roof of which can be seen here. *AEB 6337*

Opposite Bottom: Whilst a DMU waits in the bay platform, Hymek Class 35 No. D7009 has brought in a service from Bristol on 3rd August 1965. The lengthy island platform provided here was a reminder of former busy times and was seldom needed to its full extent as traffic dwindled and 3, 2 or latterly just single car DMUs sufficed. The line remains open into the 21st Century, being one of the few remnants of Bristol's once extensive suburban network. *AS S95-2*

Subsoil: marl. Beach: pebbly.
Penarth's great asset is its situation on a headland jutting into the Bristol Channel, with a splendid public park on the cliffs giving wide views across the sea to the coasts of Devon and Somerset. Turner House, which is under the control of the National Museum of Wales, contains many of Turner's paintings and a large collection of porcelain.

PENARTH FOR PLEASURE OR HEALTH VISIT THIS CHARMING SOUTH WALES RESORT

SWIMMING : PLEASURE BOAT CRUISES : DELIGHTFUL WALKS
FISHING : TENNIS : GOLF AND BOWLS : CINEMAS AND DANCES
OFFICIAL GUIDE FREE FROM CLERK OF THE COUNCIL

By the 1970s, this image dating from 24th March 1973, Penarth was but a shadow of its former self. Following closure of the line west of Penarth to Lavernock, Sully, Cadoxton and Barry in May 1968, the station became the terminus of a truncated single line from Cardiff. The majority of the station buildings seen here on the surviving operational platform were demolished as part of a remodelling in 1974. The branch still sees a healthy level of commuter traffic into the Welsh capital however, with 619,000 passenger journeys recorded in 2019/20.

BARRY ISLAND

Population 38,000. Subsoil: limestone. Climate: bracing. Marine Lake and open air swimming bath. Pleasure steamers.

Barry Island is the playground of South Wales – a glorious beach of sand enclosed by grass topped headlands with a big amusement park where the cliffs sink to the level of the shore in the centre of Whitmore Bay. The big scenic railway, immediately outside Barry Island station, is always an attraction. Public gardens have been laid out and a miniature golf course, concert hall, open air dancing floors, dance halls, cinemas and the largest open air swimming bath in Wales, with sunbathing gardens, have been provided.

Above: An unidentified 5600 Class 0-6-2T, with the relatively new "British Railways" on its side tanks, is captured here leaving Barry Island station in this June 1949 view hauling the empty stock of an excursion to this popular seaside resort. Perhaps of equal interest are the occupants of the adjoining road with a Brylcreemed cyclist to the fore, a motorcyclist and passenger (sans helmets of course), a venerable automobile (any colour as long as it's black) and single and double deck buses completing this nostalgic picture of transport of the late 1940s. *JCF G6-4 6/49*

Below: Drawing its coaching stock out of one of the berthing sidings provided to the left of this view taken on 24th. August 1960, 5100 Class No. 4151 prepares to enter Barry Island station. The roof of the diesel car servicing facility, DMUs having been introduced on local services in 1958, can just be made out above the carriage roofs of the train and off to the right past the balloon water tower lies the entrance to the tunnel taking the line down the grade to Barry Pier station. The long excursion platform can be seen on the right whilst the elegant terrace of villas in Plymouth Road is evident on the left. *PY10006BA*

To give improved passenger access to the P. & A. Campbell's White Funnel steamers that plied the Bristol Channel, the line was extended from Barry Island in 1899 through a 280-yard tunnel to a new Barry Pier station seen here on 24th August 1962 with one of the aforementioned Campbell's paddle steamers tied up at the pontoon. In addition to the sloping ramp seen by the main station building, a hydraulic lift was provided at the far end of the platform to convey passengers from the station to the pontoon. The last steamer, the "Balmoral", called here in October 1971 and train services from Barry Pier station run in connection with sailings finished on the 12th of that month. The final train, a special excursion, ran in April 1973; however the pier station was not officially closed until July 1976. *PY10191B*

PORTHCAWL

Beaches: five large - sandy. Climate: dry and sunny.
Porthcawl's splendid situation, on a promontory jutting out into the Severn Sea, ensures an ozone laden atmosphere as exhilarating as if it were an island but with none of the disadvantages of being cut off from the mainland. Its splendid sand dunes rise to a height of over 200 feet and its vast stretch of golden sands is the joy of children and bathers. With a splendid record for sunshine and a mild climate, Porthcawl's reputation among holiday makers is secure.

PORTHCAWL—GLAMORGAN

Ideal Situation. Southern Aspect. No Climbing. Sea-girt Lock's Common of 70 acres. Safe Bathing. Bracing Air on Western side. Calm and restful conditions at the Newton End. Mountainous background with shelter from North and East winds. Tennis, Bowls, Golf. Amusement Park. Continuous Programme at Grand Pavilion. Riding Schools. Children's Bathing Pool. Facilities for Sea-fishing. Channel Cruises during Summer Season. First-class Hotels and Boarding Houses.

For Official Guide apply to :—
The Clerk, Council Offices, Porthcawl, Glam.   Tel. : 194.

Below: At the height of the 1958 holiday season, 9th. August to be exact, 4500 Class prairie tank No. 5555 stands at Porthcawl terminus under the admiring gaze of a couple of boys, one sporting his smart school uniform, whilst a member of the footplate crew makes his way along the platform. A luggage trolley well stocked with suitcases, possibly being consigned under the PLA (Passengers Luggage in Advance) scheme which allowed holidaymakers to send their luggage on ahead without being encumbered with it during their journey, is evident under the canopy. This 3¾ mile branch from the main line at Pyle saw eight departures daily in 1958 with some being through services to Swansea, Newport, Cardiff and Bridgend. The branch closed five years later in September 1963. *AEB3887*

West Wales

FERRYSIDE
Safe bathing. Early Closing: Wednesday.
The modern houses and bungalows of Ferryside are set among trees on the shores of the estuary of the Towy, near where it flows into Carmarthen Bay. It is linked by a ferry to Llanstephan. Ferryside's fine sands make it an attractive place for a quiet open air holiday.

Above: Holidaymakers at Ferryside, including a couple of young ladies in their summer frocks and a young family with a toddler in a pram, waiting for a service in the Carmarthen direction, have the opportunity to observe Castle Class No. 5016 "Montgomery Castle" clatter through the station with an up milk train. Milk was an important commodity in this part of the world and was regularly conveyed to the capital by fast freight services. Whitland was the main collecting point and Acton in West London the main recipient depot. Such express locomotives as Castles and Kings were often used to pull these very heavy trains at speed in order to keep time delays with this perishable cargo to a minimum. *NS201184*

Below: Rumbling through Ferryside at a somewhat more sedate pace comes No. 5549 at the head of an assorted rake of wagons on an unrecorded date. On the right behind the station fence a mother holds on firmly to her excited, or perhaps apprehensive, child who had possibly never seen such a noisy frightening spectacle before. Also on the right is one of the popular Camp Coaches sited to take advantage of the views afforded by the location of the station next to the broad estuary of the River Towy. *NS201198*

TENBY
Population 4,500. Aspect: South-south-west. Altitude: 80 to 200 feet above sea level.

Tenby has exceptional attractions as a family resort where the tastes of each individual member of the family can be gratified. There are splendid sands, rocks, caves and islands for the children, all kinds of sports, cinemas, dances and entertainments for the adults, quiet nooks on the cliffs or amongst the sand dunes for those in need of a restful holiday, an outstandingly interesting 13th century parish church, 14th century city walls, a Tudor house and the remains of a medieval castle for the historically minded, and a delightful variety of walks and rides for the energetic.

On 1st June 1961 Carmarthen based Manor Class No. 7804 "Baydon Manor" waits at Tenby with, if the station clock is correct, the 10:33 am departure for Pembroke Dock whilst the signalman returns to his cabin carrying the pouch. This service provided a connection at Whitland from the 8:00 am service from Swansea to Neyland. The ornate station covered footbridge dating from 1896 is a particularly attractive feature of this location but, like so many others, this was later replaced with a modern uncovered concrete structure. *LRF6014*

Top: Premier train of the line was undoubtedly the "Pembroke Coast Express", which had been inaugurated as late as 1953, seen here in this undated view at Tenby hauled by Manor Class No. 7829 "Ramsbury Manor" proudly displaying the headboard. The locomotive is carrying an 87G shed code indicating it was based at Carmarthen. This restaurant car service from Paddington ran non-stop to Newport thence calling at Swansea, Llanelly, Carmarthen, St. Clears and Whitland before traversing the Tenby branch, reaching Pembroke Dock 6½ hours after leaving the capital. The "Pembroke Coast Express" name was discontinued in 1963. Notice the ornate footbridge has been replaced by a concrete version which itself was to be further replaced by today's welded steel structure. The large advertising hoarding seen on the far right was for George Ace Ltd., a garage in the town selling amongst other marques Wolseley cars. George Ace had been an amateur cycling champion in his time, winning the title Amateur Cycling champion of Wales & Monmouthshire in 1879. He opened a cycle shop near the station in Tenby and later dealt in cars. He died in 1941 but his son kept his memory alive, running the garage that bore his name. *NS201197C*

Bottom: The aforementioned Ace's Cycle & Motor Works can be seen to the rear of the modern Tenby signal box which dated from 1956 when it replaced the original wooden box of 1895. The new box closed in 1988 and these days there are self-service electric token release facilities for drivers giving permission to proceed, Tenby being the only passing place on the single track route from Whitland to Pembroke Dock. *LRF6032 01.06.61*

Mid Wales

CARDIGAN
Golf (9 holes). Early closing: Wednesday.

Cardigan, on the banks of the River Teifi which forms the boundary between Cardiganshire and Pembrokeshire, is not only the county town but an excellent touring centre offering river boating, bathing and fishing with sea bathing at Gwbert-on-sea, 2½ miles away. It is at St. Dogmael's, at the mouth of the Teifi, that the few remaining coracle men can be found carrying on the tradition of salmon fishing in round coracles exactly similar to those first used by the ancient Britons over 1,000 years ago.

On 2nd June 1961, in addition to a handful of passengers, there appears to be plenty of parcels and mailbags to be unloaded from the recent arrival of 4500 Class prairie tank No. 5549 at Cardigan. According to the shed code carried by the locomotive it was officially allocated to 87H Neyland which had sub sheds at Cardigan, Milford Haven, Pembroke Dock and Whitland. There was a small locomotive shed at the terminus which was demolished after closure although the station building survived for a time as offices for an agricultural equipment supplier. Terminus of the branch from the main line at Whitland, the sparse service of three or four trains each way daily was by this date hopelessly uneconomic and it was no surprise that, with a journey time of 1¾ hours for just 27½ miles, closure came just over a year later in September 1962. *H2433*

Taken one day before the previous image, on 1st June 1961, this view shows No. 5520, having run round its train, ready to couple up for the return journey to Whitland, scheduled to leave at 5:45 pm. The running in board, attractive white stone bordered flower beds and the small platform end signal box which had a frame of 12 levers and was staffed until the end of services, which of course did nothing for the economics of the line, all add to the interest of the scene. The terminus was sited near the banks of the River Teifi which can just be seen to the left of the locomotive. Today an industrial estate covers the site. *LRF6051*

ABERYSTWYTH

Aspect: south and due west. Beach: pebbles and sand. Excellent fishing in the Rivers Teifi, Rheidol and Dovey, also the Angling Association's lakes.

Aberystwyth is the largest resort in Mid Wales. The view from Constitution Hill, easily reached by a footpath or by cliff railway, and embracing the whole of Cardigan Bay and its encircling mountains, would alone be sufficient to account for the popularity of Aberystwyth as a holiday and tourist centre, but the town has far more to offer – hotels and boarding houses to suit every taste and purse.

On an unrecorded date in 1960 Manor Class No. 7826 "Longworth Manor" has charge of a service from Aberystwyth to Carmarthen. Just three services daily were provided on this 56¼ mile route which passed through sparsely populated country with Lampeter and Pencader being the only significant settlements. Although five of the intermediate twenty-one stations were request stops, it still took nearly two and half hours to traverse the line leading to an average speed of just 23 mph. The route formally closed on 22nd February 1965 although floods had closed the section between Aberystwyth and Strata Florida prematurely on 14th December 1964. *NS201183*

Opposite Top: This 1948 view of Dukedog No. 9065 "Tre Pol & Pen" at Aberystwyth reveals a locomotive which had an interesting history. In December 1929 Duke Class No.3265 "Tre Pol & Pen" was withdrawn and the cab and other above-frame fittings together with a spare Duke boiler and smokebox were fitted to the straight-topped frames of Bulldog No. 3365 "Charles Grey Mott". The rebuilt locomotive continued to carry the original name of No. 3265 and this conversion resulted in locomotives with stronger frames which could still be used on yellow weight restricted routes and thus were able to work over the wooden Barmouth bridge which helped to ensure their longevity on former Cambrian Railways lines into the late 1950s. The conversion was judged to be a success and from 1936 twenty-nine "new" locomotives were constructed from the relevant components of withdrawn Dukes and Bulldogs, becoming known as Dukedogs. The name of No. 9065 stems from the old Cornish rhyme "By Tre Pol and Pen shall ye know all Cornishmen" reflecting the fact that Cornish surnames often begin with one of these three prefixes. The locomotive seen here was not to last much longer as it was withdrawn after a service life of some 53 years at the end of 1949. *NS200149*

Opposite Bottom: More modern motive power is evident here in this view of a Class 108 DMU with DTSL (Driver Trailer Second Lavatory) M56264 leading this 2 car set at Aberystwyth on 16th April 1966. Built at Derby Works in late 1959 and known as "Derby Lightweights" due to their aluminium construction, this unit lasted in service until 1992 being subsequently scrapped at Booth Roe Metals of Rotherham. Above the left buffer the depot code LW reveals that it was based at Birmingham's Lawley Street depot at this time. DMUs had first arrived at Aberystwyth back in September 1957 and by 1965 they had taken over most services except for the "Cambrian Coast Express" and certain night mail trains. Steam finished completely in this area on 4th March 1967 and DMUs still provide the bulk of services today albeit with modern Class 158 units. AS U29-2

Above: No mention of Aberystwyth would be complete without including a view of one of the Vale of Rheidol (VoR) tank locomotives, the trio of which achieved fame as BR's final steam locomotives following the cessation of steam on the national network in August 1968. This view of No.9 "Prince of Wales" dates from 29th June 1962 when the VoR locomotives were still confined to their own shed prior to assuming occupation of the former GWR shed in May 1968 following its closure. The green livery also predates the absurd decision to paint the trio in BR blue with large arrow symbols. The narrow gauge 4 ton wagons of loco coal and the water tower add interest to the scene. BR subsequently disposed of the VoR in 1989. *WS6199*

BORTH
Tennis: hard courts. Safe bathing.

Borth has a long standing reputation as a quiet family resort with bracing air and four miles of golden sands reaching to the estuary of the Dovey. Its situation on the shores of Cardigan Bay is a guarantee of a magnificent panorama from the beach and endless fascinating excursions in the neighbourhood.

The attractive station at Borth had been the terminus for a year or so before the line was extended to Aberystwyth and although the beach was attractive enough, the hinterland was composed mainly of marshy ground. This view dating from 31st May 1961 shows the small platform sited signal box which contained 17 levers and dated from the resignalling scheme of 1891. It was closed in November 1973 consequent upon the passing loop being taken out of service. A camping coach was sited here for a number of years and one can just be discerned in the bay in the right background. *H2366*

TOWYN

Population 3,803. Beach: shingle.
Towyn, on a wide plain sheltered by a semi circle of hills from all cold winds but open on the west to the sea, is a healthy little holiday resort which attracts ever increasing numbers of visitors. It possesses a fine promenade commanding a wonderful panorama of sea and mountains and the progressive little town is keen to add to its attractions for visitors without spoiling its quiet charm.

Right: On 28th June 1962 Class 4 No. 75021 on an up service runs in to Towyn station which like many stations in the area had the attractive "fish" motif in the decorative ironwork at the ends of the platform canopy. Sadly the canopy is no longer extant at Towyn. Over the years Machynlleth depot had a number of these useful Standard 4-6-0s on its books with several forming part of its final allocation before closure to steam traction at the end of 1966. *WS6195*

Below: Looking north from Neptune Road bridge, No. 78003 leaves Towyn for the south and rejoins the single line on an unrecorded date in the 1960s. A few wagons can be seen in the small goods yard indicating that there was still some freight traffic at this time and on the left can be seen a refuge siding, an unusual feature on Cambrian lines, having been partially relaid with concrete blocks. No. 78003 was

one of the 65 strong members of the class produced between 1952-56 but as much of the work they were intended for was rapidly disappearing they, along with many other Standard designs, did not enjoy a particularly long service life, No. 78003 lasting just 14 years before withdrawal at the end of 1966. These 2MT locomotives were considered somewhat underpowered by local footplatemen and were later replaced by Standard Class 3MT and 4MT tanks. *MP 60001*

North Wales

BARMOUTH

Beach: firm sand. Recreations: golf at Dyffryn and Fairbourne, bowls, tennis, fishing, boating, bathing and mountaineering.

No place in Great Britain is more superbly sited than Barmouth, at the seaward end of the glorious Barmouth estuary. The older part of the town has quaint by-ways climbing the mountains above the great stretch of sands. Masses of hydrangeas, fuchsias, aloes and myrtles flourish in the gardens of Barmouth, testifying to its mild and equable climate, which ensures its popularity as a health resort throughout the year. The walks along the shores of the Barmouth estuary, or by the bridge half a mile in length across the mouth of the Mawddach, give inspiring views of range upon range of mountains ringing the estuary with an ever changing play of light and shade and ever new beauties as the tide ebbs and flows.

Opposite: Two cyclists pause after having paid their tolls to cross Barmouth Viaduct as the "Cambrian Coast Express" proceeds at a stately pace headed by Dukedog No. 9014 which was to be withdrawn in October 1960. The milepost signifies 100 miles from Whitchurch where the Cambrian Railways lines from the Cardigan Bay resorts joined the main London & North Western Railway route from Shrewsbury to Crewe. The "Honesty Toll" today for pedestrians is £1 for adults and 50p for children - back in the late 1950s it was probably pence. The coaches are emerging from the 70 yard long Barmouth tunnel seen in the background. The viaduct, some 800 yards long, has 113 spans and is built on over 500 piles driven into the sand of the estuary. *REV 594-3*

Above: Collett 0-6-0 No. 2255 heads south over Barmouth Bridge with the prestigious up "Cambrian Coast Express" working. The locomotive, carrying an 89C shedplate signifying Machynlleth from where it was withdrawn in May 1962, was one of the few tender classes with a light enough axle load to be permitted to cross the wooden viaduct before it was strengthened, others being the Dukedogs and Ivatt Class 2 2-6-0s. The bridge was closed during the autumn of 2021 to allow a £30m restoration scheme to proceed. Back in 1941 it had featured in the Gainsborough Pictures film "The Ghost Train", famously written by Arnold Ridley, Pte. Godfrey of Dad's Army fame. *REV 285-1*

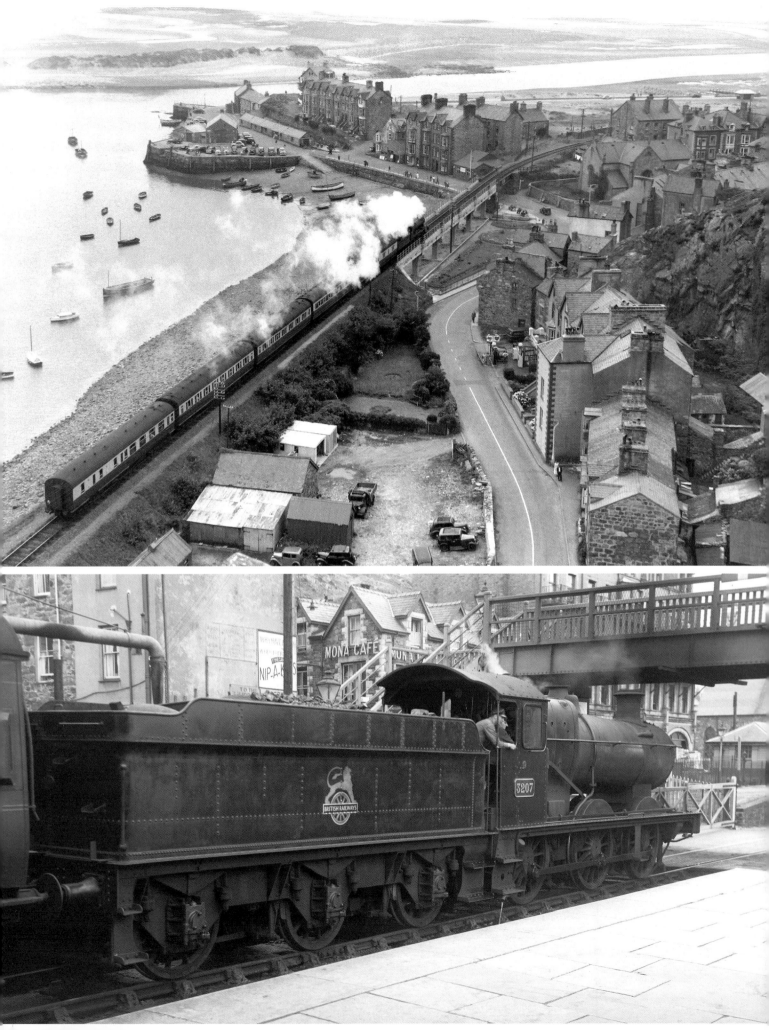

Opposite Top: The picturesque approach to Barmouth is captured in this view taken from an elevated position to the south of the town. An unidentified Collett 2200 Class with five coaches in tow crosses Old Chapel viaduct and passes the small harbour with boats lying at anchor. A motorist is having his car filled up at the local BP garage on the right, no self – service in those days, and a number of interesting vehicles of the period can be seen on the waste ground in the foreground and parked on the quay. The headroom under the metal span which crossed the road was 10' 3" and carried a suitable warning sign for high vehicles. *REV 278-2*

Opposite Bottom: Less than five years old, 2200 Class 0-6-0 No. 3207 has charge of a southbound service at Barmouth on 26th July 1951. The gates have been closed to road traffic so departure is probably imminent. Delivered new to Machynlleth depot in October 1946, the Collett remained there until transfer to Oswestry in 1955. The Mona Cafe, prominent in the background, was a favourite eatery in the town for many years but today is the Barmouth Original Welsh Rock shop. The large advertisement behind the tender is for "Nip-a-Kofs" which were apparently a black cough sweet, a popular item stocked by grocers at the time. *RCR 3275*

The Dolgelly shuttle often used the separate excursion platform at Barmouth, especially on busy summer Saturdays, to keep it out of the way of through trains and to avoid having to operate the gates guarding the adjacent level crossing. On 29th May 1961 7400 Class pannier tank No. 7417 has a two coach set ready for the 5.48 pm departure. Stock for the shuttle, which was well patronised by locals and tourists alike, was kept at Dolgelly overnight with the locomotive stabled at Penmaenpool shed. In addition to through services on the Barmouth Junction – Ruabon route, Dolgelly also enjoyed some three daily shuttle services to and from Barmouth. The loading gauge seen here was particularly important on the Cambrian Coast lines as clearances were notoriously "tight" on several sections. It was positioned here as the end of the excursion platform was often used as a loading ramp for freight traffic. *H2291*

Above: A picture full of interest as, with steam to spare, 2-6-0 No. 46433 heads past Barmouth South signal box with, as evidenced by the attractive headboard carried on the smokebox, the "Cambrian Radio Cruise" circular tour. Note the tablet catching apparatus situated adjacent to the signal box and the 5mph temporary speed restriction sign. Behind the signal box was situated the local Crosville bus office and some of the bus stops can be seen to the right of the signal post. These Ivatt locomotives, introduced in 1946, weighed in at just 47 tons so were one of the few tender classes allowed to cross Barmouth bridge. Allocated to Rhyl depot at times during 1956-58, which probably helps to date this image, this locomotive ended up in North West England at Carnforth from where it was withdrawn in 1967. A further locomotive waits at the excursion platform where coaching stock for the Dolgelly shuttle would often be parked and a fine collection of cars of the period can be seen on the waste ground to the right of the train. *REV 284-2*

Below: A close cousin of the Ivatt 2-6-0s was the Standard Class 2, sixty-five of which were produced in the 78XXX number series between 1952-56. Here doyen of the class No. 78000 departs Barmouth with a service to Machynlleth on an unrecorded date. Four members of the class are preserved but not No. 78000 which after having spent ten years allocated to Machynlleth depot from 1953 – 1963 was withdrawn from Derby in 1965 and scrapped the following year. *REV 77C 4-4*

HARLECH

Golf (18 holes) Royal St. David's Golf Club.

Harlech, famous in song and story since the Middle Ages, is scarcely less famous in the present day for its Championship Golf Course laid out on the level grassy seashore below the great cliffs on which the romantic ruins of Harlech castle are perched. Steep roads wind down from the ancient village to the golf links and to the modern villas and bungalows built by holiday makers and those who have returned to stay as permanent residents. Harlech castle is in the care of H.M. Office of Works.

Standard Class 4 No. 75020, based at Machynlleth shed, was a regular performer on the Cambrian coast lines in the early 1960s and this view of it halted at Harlech station with the 7:40 am service from Pwllheli dates from 30th. May 1961. This train, which called at all stations except Black Rock halt, obviously conveyed a large number of schoolchildren judging by the gaggle alighting and crossing the footbridge. Arrival time here was 8:42 am so the pupils will have to hurry to make morning assembly although the secondary school, these days going by the name Ysgol Ardudwy, was situated close to the station. The fine station building seen on the opposite platform still survives into the 21st Century. The locomotive lasted in service until August 1968, its final allocation being Carnforth. *LRF5913*

PORTMADOC

Climate: mild and salubrious. Plentiful supply of soft water. Subsoil: sand.

Portmadoc is a very pleasant little town in a splendid setting on the Glaslyn estuary. The great embankment which carries the road across the estuary makes a mile long promenade giving superb views of the mountains of Snowdonia. The birthplace of Lawrence of Arabia and the house in which Shelley lived for a time are still to be seen at Tremadoc, a mile away. Although the little Festiniog Railway has unfortunately fallen into disrepair, Portmadoc is still a great centre for exploring Snowdonia.

Below: With the imposing bulk of Moel-y-Gest, 263 metres in height, in the distance, Dukedog No. 9021 pulls into Portmadoc sometime in 1954 with a southbound service crossing the northbound one seen at the down platform. By the end of 1954 there were still twenty-four examples of the twenty-nine strong Dukedog class at work and, although many of them would experience long stretches in store, they lasted well into the late 1950s with the final pair going as late as October 1960. No. 9021, seen here, was withdrawn at the end of 1958. *NS201124A*

Opposite Top: Standard Class 4 No. 75020 is captured at Portmadoc on 30th May 1961 with the 7:40 am service from Pwllheli to Barmouth. A member of the station staff takes the opportunity of exchanging a few words with the footplate crew during the scheduled two minute stop here. *LRF5911*

Opposite Bottom: With its bunker piled high with coal, Standard Class 2-6-2T No. 82020 is seen at Portmadoc on 25th June 1962 with a southbound service from Pwllheli. The level crossing adjacent to the station still retains its gates in this view but today these have been replaced by lifting barriers. Having been allocated to the SR's Exmouth Junction shed from new, No. 82020 went on to see service at Nuneaton, Wrexham, Shrewsbury and Machynlleth before ending its days back on the SR at Nine Elms from where it was withdrawn in September 1965. It did finally end up back in Wales, albeit at Bird's scrapyard in Risca. *ES4479*

A pair of Class 108 DMUs in green livery with yellow warning panels await time at Portmadoc with a Machynlleth to Pwllheli local service in August 1966. Five of the six former chimneys of the main station building have now been truncated and capped whilst on the far right the water tower still survives in this post-steam world. Today of course this feature has long gone and indeed no functioning chimneys now adorn this unstaffed halt run by Transport for Wales although the platform awning still affords limited protection from the North Wales weather for waiting passengers. The spelling of the station name was changed to Porthmadog in May 1975. *FM40-2*

CRICCIETH

Golf (18 holes). Recreations: riding, tennis, bowls, miniature golf, children's playground, cinema.

Criccieth, with its picturesque castle ruins on their grassy mound dividing its two great bathing beaches, is one of those delightful seaside resorts which are half town and half village. Combining the best of each to make a happy, healthy family resort. Brynawelon, Lady Megan Lloyd George's Criccieth home, is on a hill north of the High Street, and Earl Lloyd George's unique grave can be seen 1½ miles away beside the little river at Llanystumdwy.

On 30th June 1961 Standard Class No. 75026, although not carrying a headboard, has charge of the up "Cambrian Coast Express" at Criccieth. Leaving Criccieth at a quarter past 10 in the morning and travelling via Shrewsbury and Birmingham Snow Hill, one could be in the capital by 6 o'clock in the evening. The Restaurant Car provided on this service began its journey at Aberystwyth so Criccieth passengers would have to wait until Dovey Junction, where the two portions joined, to sample its delights. *FH937*

As passengers leave the train at Criccieth this image gives us an opportunity to view one of the two Observation Cars built initially for the Southern's "Devon Belle" Pullman service. In its guise as the "Welsh Chieftain Lounge Car" it was part of one of the popular "Land Cruise" services which operated in North Wales during the 1950s with the train, as the publicity brochure remarked, being wired with "Amplifier equipped for descriptive commentary and music". The initial Land Cruise service had begun in 1951 at the time of the Festival of Britain and was named the "Festival Land Cruise". Until the final season in 1961, variations in the circular route around North Wales were tried and marketed under a variety of names such as the Cambrian Radio Cruise, North Wales Radio Land Cruise, North Wales Radio Cruise and the Welsh Chieftain, all of which carried special headboards. The route generally involved clockwise travel from Llandudno to Pwllheli via Rhyl, Corwen, Dolgelly, Barmouth, Portmadoc, Pwllheli, Caernarvon and Bangor on certain weekdays with an anti-clockwise route being followed on other days of the week. This view dates from August 1959. The Observation Car numbered 280 went on to grace West Highland metals on the Kyle of Lochalsh line and was subsequently purchased for use on the South Devon Railway where it can be seen in service today. The other former "Devon Belle" Observation Car was repatriated from the USA and is being restored on the Swanage Railway. The slating of the Corwen – Denbigh line for closure in 1961, which was in fact to prove premature as it did not close until 1965, and the subsequent banning of passenger excursions running over it effectively rendered circular tours of North Wales by rail no longer feasible. *NF 011-36 8.59*

PENYCHAIN

Penychain opened as a halt in 1933 but took on a more important role after 1940 when the Royal Navy requested Billy Butlin to convert a holiday camp which he was constructing here to a training facility in a similar vein to his facilities already requisitioned at Filey by the Admiralty. After the cessation of hostilities the camp assumed its intended role as Butlin's Pwllheli holiday camp from 1947. Renamed Starcoast World in 1990, the site was taken over by Haven Holidays in 1999 and is now predominantly a site for static caravans. Trains continue to call but only on request.

No. 5510 gets away from Penychain bound for Barmouth and the south whilst on the opposite platform a number of "happy campers" have just arrived and are making their way to the camp for a week or a fortnight's holiday, courtesy of Billy Butlin, on 18th June 1960. The station had opened as a halt in 1933 and led a fairly quiet existence until Butlin's camp was constructed nearby, originally for the Admiralty to serve a nearby training base, but in 1947 it was converted for holidaymakers and the halt was upgraded to station status with staff being provided in the summer months. The tracks through the station were signalled for bi-directional working and the route was doubled as far as Afon Wen junction where the Caernarvon and Bangor line diverged. Butlins had their own "Puffing Billy" road-going train to ferry campers from the station to the camp. These days, much reduced in size, it has reverted to halt status and serves the Haven holiday and caravan park on the former Butlins site. *JB000059*

PWLLHELI

Population 4,000. Aspect: south. Churches: various denominations.
It is an essential part of Pwllheli's fascination for visitors that it is in two distinct parts – the older town close under the hills and the "West End" beside the beach. Eastwards from the parade is a breezy expanse of grass grown sand dunes giving splendid views of the coast and the heights of Snowdonia, and curving protectingly round the vast natural harbour. The shooting obtainable in the surrounding countryside is generally acknowledged to be superlatively good. The climate wins the wholehearted commendation of the medical profession for the town is well protected from cold winds yet open to all the healing sea breezes and boasting an exceptionally high sunshine record.

Above: The exterior of Pwllheli station is seen in this view dating from 30th May 1961. At this time the station had two tracks with an island platform. In 1977 one side of the island was abandoned and the track lifted. Today part of the station building acts as a cafe whilst the remainder provides covered waiting accommodation. A single track and platform and covered concourse are all that remains today at the station, which is unstaffed. A vintage Shell petrol pump seen on the far right outside the adjacent Imperial Garage is worthy of notice. Today a waterfront bar and restaurant occupies the site of the former garage. *LRF5904*

Below: We end as we began as our final view is another old stager on her last knockings seen at the former island platform at Pwllheli terminus on 30th September 1960. Class 3200 "Dukedog" No. 9017 was one of only two class members still in service at this date and she would be withdrawn together with the other survivor, No. 9014, just one month later in October from Oswestry shed. Fortunately No. 9017 went on to a life in preservation, being in fact the subject of the first ever appeal for funds to preserve a standard gauge locomotive. Arriving on the Bluebell Railway in February 1962 it subsequently received the name "Earl of Berkeley" previously carried by Castle Class No. 5060. The 4-4-0 has been out of service since 2011 and is currently awaiting its next major overhaul. *RCR15448*